The Mission and Ministry of the Church in England

Monsignor Michael Nazir-Ali draws on the rich history of *Ecclesia Anglicana*, the complex reality that has been the English church from the beginning—he discusses its glories, achievements, vicissitudes, and failures; as well as the expansion and adaptation of this "Anglican" heritage to different parts of the world and many cultures.

Nazir-Ali starts with the different ways in which England was first evangelized and how, in turn, the Church in England (*Ecclesia Anglicana*) was able to send missionaries to continental Europe for primary evangelism and church planting. He examines the more recent past with the evangelical and Catholic revivals in the eighteenth and nineteenth centuries and their significance for mission both at home and abroad. The formation of mission agencies gave a new impetus to mission, challenging people to give, to pray, and to go. He then considers what we can learn from mission today in different parts of the world; providing specific examples of such missionary activity of the churches in Nigeria and Kenya, as well as the churches in South East Asia. He also discusses the role of the new Ordinariates in the Catholic Church which allow authentic Anglican patrimony to exist and flourish within the Catholic Church itself

The book examines how the gospel connects with culture, what we need to learn from the global Church about mission and ministry, the different models for mission and ministry, ranging from the incarnational to the itinerant, from inculturation to social and political activism and from embassy to hospitality.

The Mission and Ministry of the Church in England

History, Challenge, and Prospect

Michael Nazir-Ali

t&tclark

LONDON • NEW YORK • OXFORD • NEW DELHI • SYDNEY

T&T CLARK
Bloomsbury Publishing Plc
50 Bedford Square, London, WC1B 3DP, UK
1385 Broadway, New York, NY 10018, USA
29 Earlsfort Terrace, Dublin 2, Ireland

BLOOMSBURY, T&T CLARK and the T&T Clark logo are trademarks of
Bloomsbury Publishing Plc

First published in Great Britain 2024

Cover images: St. Augustine of Canterbury © The Picture Art Collection/Alamy
Stock Photo. Queen Bertha of Kent © Holmes Garden Photos/Alamy Stock
Photo. Mosaic of Saint Theodore © Adam Ján Figel/Alamy Stock Photo

A catalogue record for this book is available from the British Library.

A catalog record for this book is available from the Library of Congress.

ISBN: HB: 978-0-5677-1333-9
        PB: 978-0-5677-1332-2
        ePDF: 978-0-5677-1334-6
        ePUB: 978-0-5677-1335-3

Typeset by RefineCatch Limited, Bungay, Suffolk
Printed and bound in Great Britain

To find out more about our authors and books visit www.bloomsbury.com
and sign up for our newsletters.

CONTENTS

Introduction

Why This Book Was Written and What Is in It

Mission is back in fashion! Churches, clergy, and laypeople are no longer content with just pastoral and therapeutic approaches to ministry. They want the gospel—the good news of Jesus Christ incarnate, crucified, risen, and ascended, who overcame our alienation from and rebellion against God, the source of our being, and was victorious, on our behalf, over death and the devil. They want to be equipped to carry this message into their communities and beyond, making the gospel credible among the people they reach. They seek also to welcome people into their churches and at worship in ways that are attractive as well as challenging, leading those who come to commitment and discipleship.

By *Ecclesia Anglicana* I mean the complex reality that has been the English church from the beginning. Its glories, achievements, vicissitudes, and failures, as well as the expansion and adaptation of this "Anglican" heritage to different parts of the world and in many cultures. This tradition has a long and varied history of missionary engagement, awareness of which can provide us with important tools for thinking about and doing mission in our own time and place. Churches and Christians can also learn from the experience— the successes and failures—of fellow Christians from other parts of the world and other periods of history. This book is an attempt to draw on the rich story of *Ecclesia Anglicana*, from the earliest times to our own, so that we can be inspired and lessons can be learned, good practice emulated, and past mistakes avoided.

The first chapter deals with the different ways in which England was first evangelized and how, in turn, the Church of (or in) England (*Ecclesia Anglicana*) was able to send missionaries to continental Europe for primary evangelism and church planting. There is consideration here of the different ways in which the missionaries approached the peoples and cultures they encountered. These have important lessons for us today.

We move on then to the impact that the preaching orders, the Dominicans, and the Franciscans had on spiritual life in England, giving the people a taste for hearing sermons at a time when many parish clergy were unable or unwilling to preach. Next, we look at the Reformation and its peculiarly Anglican character, with both continuity and reform, with a return to a serious study of the Bible but also with bishops in historic succession and with worship in the vernacular, which also drew on the Fathers and the early church. What were the missionary implications of the Anglican Reformers' desire to disciple the nation and why was there an absence of awareness about the need for engaging in world mission? Was the aim of those who remained in obedience to Rome simply to survive, or did they also want to persuade their compatriots to be reconciled to the church, as they understood it, of their forefathers? The chapter concludes by asking whether there were any seeds of a missionary understanding of the church sown in the sixteenth and seventeenth centuries which were to bear fruit in the eighteenth and nineteenth centuries.

This brings us to Chapter 2, where we examine the more recent past with the evangelical and Catholic revivals in the eighteenth and nineteenth centuries and their significance for mission both at home and abroad. The formation of mission agencies gave a new impetus to mission, challenging people to give, to pray, and to go. The debates between evangelicals and Anglo-Catholics about the best way to plant churches, the role of bishops as missionaries and pastors, and how culture is to be handled, all have a particularly Anglican ring to them. There were those particularly, but not only, from the Catholic revival in the Church of England who were reconciled to the Catholic Church. After Catholic emancipation (1829) and the restoration of the hierarchy (1850), did the Catholic Church seek the "conversion" of England?

With this varied history behind us, we go on in Chapter 3 to consider what we can learn from mission today in different parts of the world. We mark the way in which the church in Nigeria has engaged in mission in the hardest-to-reach parts of the country and how bishops in those parts are seen primarily as leading in mission rather than simply as chief pastors of the flock, important as that is. We learn also from the way in which the church in Kenya is trying to reach nomadic populations in the north by contextualizing not only evangelistic approaches but also the very life of the church, its worship, and its ways of learning and living together. These attempts at contextualization are then related to the fundamental teaching of the churches and the warrant they can provide for such endeavor.

From Africa, we move to Asia and look at the phenomenal growth of the church, including its Anglican expression in South-East Asia, and the desire of Christians there to engage in cross-cultural mission in the region and beyond it. We then consider the immensely difficult task of mission by Christians in the Islamic world and the virtues of persistence and boldness when the going gets tough but also the surprising fruit which is sometimes obtained. This leads us to a different kind of "stony ground": mission in many parts of the Western world today and how the global lessons we have learned can be of use in addressing the mission needs of the West. We shall, of course, return to this topic in other parts of the book as well.

We are now at a point where we can begin to consider the different aspects of mission as first set out in an earlier work of mine, *From Everywhere to Everywhere: A World View of Christian Mission.*[1] This will involve us in looking at typical strengths in mission of *Ecclesia Anglicana*, such as a commitment to incarnational local presence, but also the Celtic model of itinerancy, which has been so important in the renewal and growth of the church on many occasions. We will reflect carefully on the gospel's relationship to culture and context as well, on both the opportunities for making the gospel understood and the dangers of compromise and syncretism. We will ask why evangelism is a necessary part of mission, what authentic evangelism is and is not, and how we can engage in it as churches and as Christians.

---

[1]Michael Nazir-Ali, *From Everywhere to Everywhere: A World View of Christian Mission* (London: Collins, 1991).

Where presence is concerned, we will look in Chapter 4 at the parish church, as a historic example of it, but also at other modes of presence, such as chaplaincies, religious communities, and even lone apostolic figures who have remained in sometimes dangerous situations for the sake of the gospel.

If the church, understood as the body of Christ, leads to an incarnational model of mission, seeing it as a pilgrim church, on its way to its heavenly home, helps us, in Chapter 5, to see mission as dynamic (1 Pet. 1:1; 2:11). The Gospels portray Jesus as constantly on the move, and so also the apostles there and in the rest of the New Testament. It seems that a peripatetic ministry was as important in the early church as a resident one, and this complementarity is often seen in the church's story. Embassy (that is, going out) and hospitality (that is, welcoming in) are twin aspects of the one mission of the church and need equal attention from us.

How the gospel connects with culture, which aspects of it are affirmed by it and which judged, what makes for ease of transmission, and where are the blockages, all of these are perennial questions related to the church's missionary engagement with people of every culture and language. In Chapter 6, we see that both the Bible and fundamental ecclesial sources provide sufficient warrant for such engagement with culture, including its religious aspect, which is so often at its center. However, in Chapter 7, we shall ask how far we can go with inculturation, what are the various ways in which we engage in dialogue, and how its fruits are to be harvested for the sake of better understanding, faithful witness, the building of cohesive communities, and for upholding freedom of religion and belief.

This leads, in Chapter 8, to a consideration of the church's prophetic ministry of *forthtelling*—that is, speaking gospel truth to power, and of *foretelling*—that is, pointing out the consequences both of living according to God's life-giving plan for human beings and human societies and of ignoring, or even opposing, what the Creator has provided for human flourishing, even in a fallen and imperfect world. We think critically of social teaching as it has developed in different Christian traditions. We look at the way in which "Integral Mission" has come to the fore in holding together evangelization, social responsibility, and human development where none of these is neglected and, in many situations, one leads to the others.

Given the different facets of mission, we ask then in Chapter 9 why intentional evangelism remains necessary and why any discussion of mission is incomplete without it. We consider the role individual Christians and families have to play in the evangelistic task of the church but also the central importance of the congregation as the place, the means, and the engine of evangelization in its own setting and surroundings. Some pointers are provided as to how this may be done. Church planting is often seen as part of our witnessing and discipling work, and we attend to both the opportunities and the pitfalls encountered in the process of planting churches. We finish the chapter with some practical consideration of what we can do in terms of effective presence, reaching out, and welcoming. How people can be witnessed to and taught the basics of the Christian faith and life. How vocation to missionary engagement can be discerned and where to find resources to help our people engage in mission in all its wholeness.

The emergence of the Ordinariate as a particular way of being Catholic which maintains all that is of value in the Anglican tradition has, obviously, been created for those Anglicans who desire full communion with the See of Peter. Does it, however, also have an apologetic and missionary dimension in appealing, more widely, to English cultural, intellectual, and spiritual life as an authentic way of being Christian?

Finally, in Chapter 11, we bring all these threads together in a final summarizing conclusion. What Paul says of his mission is true also of every Christian, of every congregation, and of the whole church: "For if I preach the gospel, that gives me no ground for boasting because necessity is laid upon me. Woe to me if I do not preach the gospel!" (1 Cor. 9:16).

1

Ecclesia Anglicana

The Beginnings of Mission and Evangelization

The story of *Ecclesia Anglicana* is steeped in mission and evangelization. How the underground gospel of the church of the first centuries, persecuted in both the Roman and the Persian empires, arrived in Britain remains, not surprisingly, shrouded in mystery. From its shadowy beginnings with the martyrdom of Alban to hints in Tertullian and Origen suggesting the faith had reached Britain, that is about all we have. Perhaps we can add to this the attendance of British bishops at church councils and the arrival of missionary bishops from the Continent, like Germanus and Lupus, who renewed the church and evangelized pagans in the fifth century.[1]

The pagan Anglo-Saxon invaders who followed all but destroyed this church, pushing the ancient Britons, who had not been killed or assimilated, into the Welsh mountains or the Cornish peninsula. There the church continued to survive, as it did in southern Scotland, but the rest of the land was engulfed in darkness. By the end of the sixth century, the stage was set for a fresh wave of evangelization, and this was to come from both the south and the north.

---

[1] On the early period, see J. R. H. Moorman, *A History of the Church in England*, 3rd edition (London: A&C Black, 1976), 3.

Whether or not Pope Gregory the Great saw Anglo-Saxon boys being sold in the slave market in Rome, leading him to exclaim, "*Angli sunt, Angeli fiant!*" ("They are Angles, let them become Angels!"), he seems to have bought their freedom to nurture them in the Christian faith and to send them back as missionaries to their own country. When Gregory sent Augustine to England in 596, we can wonder how many of the thirty-nine monks who accompanied him had been drawn from the ranks of these young English men.[2]

Like many others after them, Augustine and his band were fearful of the fierce pagan culture to which they were being sent and tried to withdraw. However, Gregory encouraged them to persevere, and Augustine was surprised to find that the way had been prepared for him by the Christian Queen Bertha, wife of the still-pagan King Ethelbert. In the end, he was welcomed and given a listening ear. Very soon, thousands of Ethelbert's subjects were being baptized, and the king himself became the first Christian English king. Augustine's companions, who were later augmented with others, established themselves in Kent, with Rochester being the second bishopric to be founded after Canterbury. They then went on into the lands of the East Saxons, with the re-founding of the bishopric of London. One of them, Paulinus, was to go all the way to York and Northumbria to evangelize the kingdom there. He was so successful that the king, the pagan priests, and the Witan (or royal council) were all quickly converted, and Paulinus was made archbishop over the area. It was only when the newly converted King Edwin was killed by the pagans that Paulinus had to flee back to the south, to Rochester, where he became the bishop in 633. Only James the Deacon was left in Northumbria until Oswald became king and restored Christianity to his kingdom.

This time, however, it was not in its Roman form, brought over by Augustine and his monks, but the Celtic Christianity of Iona, established there by the greatest of the Irish missionaries, Columba. Iona sent Aidan to be the bishop, along with monks from Iona. In a strong partnership with King Oswald, Aidan set about evangelizing the north. The monastery he founded on Lindisfarne, which came to be called "Holy Island," sent missionaries all over England, even

---

[2]Anton Wessels, *Europe: Was it Ever Really Christian?* (London: Student Christian Ministry, 1994), 11; Stephen Neill, *A History of Christian Missions* (Harmondsworth: Penguin, 1986), 58.

as far as the Thames Estuary on the very threshold of Augustine's territory! It was also from here that the Midlands were evangelized, and the name of Chad, Bishop of Lichfield, readily comes to mind. His brother Cedd, on the other hand, was an evangelist in the east of England. When the bishops and people of the Celtic tradition accepted the Romanizing of the church at the Synod of Whitby (664), it was for the sake of Catholic unity. They did not wish to be left high and dry with their insular ecclesiology but wished to be part of the church worldwide and across the ages. Their huge contribution, however, to the primary evangelization of many parts of Britain should not be forgotten. Their model of mission, *peregrinatio*, or itineration, where bands of evangelists travel from place to place, sharing the faith and planting churches, is reminiscent of Paul's missionary journeys and has important lessons for us in this global and highly mobile age. As we shall see, presence in particular localities became typical of mission and ministry in England and has its own value, but the "pilgrim-missioners" of the north show us how to travel light and be willing to bear the hardships of the road in the task of evangelization.[3]

England was evangelized, then, from both the south and the north, by Celtic Christians from Iona and the Romanizing mission from Augustine and his successors. Whilst those of Roman usage were marked by their prioritization of organization, stability, and order, the Celts were dynamic and mobile, if somewhat unorganized. An enduring question raised by the dispute between the Celts and the Romanizers has been whether Roman forms of organization belong to the essence of catholicity or whether they are simply one way of expressing it. It is interesting, however, to note that when England began to send out missionaries to the continent, they came from a newly Romanized church but their methods of evangelization included the Celtic habit of peregrination.

No one was more of a Romanizer than Wilfred, bishop of York, Lichfield, and Hexham, yet on his way to appeal to the Pope against the Archbishop of Canterbury, Theodore of Tarsus' high-handed division of his diocese into three, Wilfred adopted the ways of an itinerant monk in carrying out primary evangelization among the

---

[3]On all of this, see the Venerable Bede, *The Ecclesiastical History of the English People* (Oxford: Oxford University Press, 2008), 37; Moorman, *History of the Church in England*, 15.

Frisians and, later, back in England, among the West Saxons. Willibrord was a pupil of both Wilfrid and of his opponents, the Irish monks. In his evangelization of the Netherlands, he adopted some of the itinerant and miracle-working ways of the *peregrini* but did not forget the need for ecclesial organization he had learned from Roman ways.

Perhaps the greatest of the Anglo-Saxon missionaries was the martyr Winfrith Boniface, the apostle to Germany. He, too, was exposed to the Celtic as well as the Roman traditions. Again, he seems to have combined missionary journeys to evangelize the pagan Germanic tribes with church planting and the wider organization of the church in Germany. It has been justly said that he, and his Anglo-Saxon companions, did more to change the face of Western Europe than anyone else.[4] If the eighth century was noted for the missions to the Germanic peoples, in the tenth century, the English church was able to assist in the evangelization of Scandinavia. The names of many of the English missionaries of this period are unknown, but their work was well-done and served the churches and the nations there effectively for many years to come.[5]

Christianity and Culture

One question that kept recurring from the time of Augustine onward was the relationship of the Christian faith and of the church to pre-Christian, pagan culture. Gregory the Great, in his advice to Augustine and his companions, can be read as being an advocate of as much continuity as possible. Thus, regarding the shrines of the pagan English, he tells Augustine not to destroy but to purify them so that they can be used for Christian worship. As for the custom of pagan sacrifices, he advises that Christian festivals should be substituted for them. In the Christianization of the culture, he favors a step-by-step approach. This has had lasting implications for English Christianity with its emphasis on continuity of buildings, worship, church order, and ecclesiastical culture generally. I sometimes wonder whether the great interest taken in maintaining

---

[4]See Wessels, *Europe: Was it Ever Really Christian?*, 96; Moorman, *History of the Church in England*, 34.
[5]Moorman, *History of the Church in England*, 44.

the continuity of buildings, even by those who never go to church, is a vestige of the folk memory about these "sacred sites" perhaps predating the Christian era.[6]

Boniface, on the other hand, took an entirely different approach. He realized that the pagan customs of the Germanic tribes held them in thrall to their gods and they needed to be liberated from such bondage. He cut down sacred trees and destroyed pagan temples and the idols within. When the Christian missionaries were not punished by the gods for their "sacrilege," the Germans realized that Jesus Christ was more powerful than their gods and accepted the Christian faith. Wessels explains that the conversion of the Germanic tribes was very much due to this power encounter with Christ and his representatives.[7]

The relation of gospel to culture has remained a live question for the churches throughout the ages. It arises in a particularly sharp form because of *Ecclesia Anglicana*'s relationship with the state, which dates to Saxon times, and because of a traditional commitment to an incarnational presence in society. To what extent can the gospel affirm and tolerate cultural practices and when must it resist and even oppose them? Sometimes an Augustinian approach will be appropriate, but at other times a Boniface will be needed. Discernment is required about what response is necessary in particular circumstances.

The Impact of Preaching Orders

From early in the thirteenth century, a new spiritual and intellectual force began to make itself felt throughout Western Europe. The secular clergy were unable to cope with the new world that was emerging, and the cloisters were inaccessible to those in the street. The emergence of the Dominican and Franciscan friars, albeit in different ways, was a response to this situation. They were called not to a parochial ministry, nor yet to prayer and contemplation in the cloisters, but to preaching the gospel in the towns and villages and to establish a presence in the newly emerging centers of learning, the universities. The friars concentrated on preaching at a time

---

[6]Bede, *Ecclesiastical History of the English People*, 57.
[7]Wessels, *Europe: Was it Ever Really Christian?*, 102, 154.

when this was a rare event in the parish churches. Wherever they went, they made their influence felt and were a powerful force in the teaching and renewal of the faith. Their itinerant missionary activities were hugely popular in England and provided models for later itinerancy.[8]

The Dominican and Franciscan mission was by no means confined to Western Europe – it ranged far and wide. The Franciscans were at the court of the Great Khans of the Mongols, where Nestorian missionaries had preceded them. The Franciscans were followed by the Dominicans. Both orders were also involved in mission to the Muslim world, and there were many martyrs.[9] The Council of Vienne, at the urging of Ramon Lull, the great scholar, missionary, and martyr, established a college in Oxford, and four other European universities, for the study of the languages of the Muslim world. During this period, we know of friars in England engaging with the Muslim world, and it is highly likely that some of them took part in the worldwide missionary activities of their orders.[10]

The Reformation

The Reformation, when it was started by Martin Luther in 1517, was not a single but a whole series of events which had the most dramatic consequences for Europe and, eventually, for the wider world. New learning, led by scholars like Erasmus, was seeking to go back to the original sources of the Scriptures. There was a desire among many of the newly literate to read the Bible for themselves. The standard of education of the parochial clergy was low and could not satisfy people's thirst for knowledge. While popular piety remained strong, even Catholic "reformers" like Erasmus and Sir Thomas More, were increasingly critical of it. Many were no longer content with knowledge of the faith passed on to them, without question, but wished to investigate for themselves and to find fresh

---

[8]Moorman, *History of the Church in England*, 102.
[9]Neill, *History of Christian Missions*, 99; Jean-Marie Gaudeul, *Encounters and Clashes: Islam and Christianity in History*, vol. 1 (Rome: Pontifical Institute for the Study of Arabic and Islamic Studies, 1984), 137.
[10]Neill, *History of Christian Missions*, 116.

assurance for their faith from its very sources. As we shall see, the shortcomings of the Reformation were very significant but we cannot neglect what it achieved in terms of translation of the Bible into the vernacular, the participation of the laity in public worship, and in its emphasis on prayer and living the Christian life.

The Anglican Reformation was certainly influenced by the Reformers in Europe, but it was also conservative: liturgical worship, albeit in the vernacular and with a new emphasis on Scripture, was retained, as was the threefold ministry of bishops, priests, and deacons in historic succession. The ambition of the Reformers was to disciple a nation hitherto ignorant of important aspects of their faith. Thomas Cranmer, the first reformed Archbishop of Canterbury (1489–1556), wanted to engage all the faculties of the worshiper in his or her worship. Hence the emphasis on "hearing" God's word, as well as reading it. Much of the beautiful language of the *Book of Common Prayer* is designed for the hearer and not the officiant alone. In the Eucharistic context, Holy Communion is given to the faithful with the exhortation to eat and to drink the body and blood of Christ and to feed on him by faith with thanksgiving. The signing with the cross at baptism, the laying on of hands at confirmation and ordination, standing, kneeling, etc. during worship, all engage the senses. The principle could, of course, be extended and, in due course of time, was extended to cover other aspects of ritual.

Yet many modern scholars fault the churches of the Reformation for lacking missionary zeal. First, the Magisterial, as opposed to the Radical, Reformation survived because of the doctrine of *Cuius regio, eius religio* ("the religion of a territory will be that of the prince").[11] As Stephen Neill points out, this meant that the pastoral concern of the church was largely limited to the domains of the ruler in whose territory it found itself. "Watch your doorstep" was the cry and it was widely heeded. For Neill, such a church could not be fully missionary. This was, indeed, the charge made against the Reformation by Roman Catholic polemicists such as Robert Bellarmine: the Protestants could make people heretics but they

---

[11]On the distinction between "magisterial" and "radical," see Owen Chadwick, *The Reformation* (London: Penguin, 1990), 189 and passim. On the Reformers' mission to disciple nations through Bible reading and worship, see Ashley Null, "Divine Allurement: Thomas Cranmer and Tudor Church Growth," in *Towards a Theology of Church Growth*, ed. David Goodhew (Farnham: Ashgate, 2015), 197–216.

could not convert the heathen.[12] Apart from *Cuius regio*, it is sometimes said that the churches of the Reformation could not engage in world mission because the sea routes were controlled either by Roman Catholic powers, like Spain and Portugal, or still by Muslims. Moreover, Protestants had to fight for their very survival and had to struggle not only with Catholic hostility but also with other Protestants. All of this may be true but, as Gustav Warneck, the great mission historian, points out, no sorrow was expressed about the inability to engage in mission. For him, the strange silence can be satisfactorily accounted for only by the fact that the recognition of the missionary obligation was itself absent. It was not just action but the very idea of world mission that was absent.[13]

In addition to the political and geographic reasons which are given for the absence of missionary thinking in the churches of the Reformation, doctrinal reasons were offered as to why churches should not engage in world mission. A curious kind of dispensationalism asserted that the command to preach the gospel to all nations had been fulfilled in the time of the apostles! Some nations had accepted this offer of salvation, while others had not. There was now no need to preach a second time to those who had not. Such dispensational thinking was related to the frequent emphasis in Reformed circles on God's sovereignty. The kingdom of God could not be extended by human effort but was the work of God alone. Even those who believed that God used earthly means in the fulfilling of his sovereign will still thought that the absence of such means for one group and their availability for another was an indication of God's will to which we must submit rather than challenge.[14] Another explanation for a lack of vision for missions beyond the territories of Protestant rulers was the perceived practical need to thoroughly disciple the people and the popular culture of those areas and to move them away from their previous piety.

---

[12]See further in Neill, *History of Christian Missions*, 188.
[13]G. Warneck, *Outline of a History of Protestant Missions from the Reformation to the Present Time: A Contribution to Modern Church History* (New York: Fleming H. Revell, 1901), 8–14.
[14]See Michael Nazir-Ali, *From Everywhere to Everywhere: A World View of Christian Mission* (London: Collins, 1991), 43; Neill, *History of Christian Missions*, 189.

There were exceptions, of course. Adapted from the medieval liturgy, one of Cranmer's Collects for Good Friday specifically prays for the conversion of the heathen:

> Merciful God, who hast made all men, and hatest nothing that thou hast made, nor wouldest the death of a sinner, but rather that he should be converted and live: have mercy upon all Jews, Turks, Infidels and Heretics, and take from them all ignorance, hardness of heart, and contempt of thy word. And so fetch them home, blessed Lord, to thy flock, that they may be saved among the remnant of the true Israelites, and be made one fold under one shepherd, Jesus Christ our Lord: who liveth and reigneth. &c.[15]

There is no evidence, however, that the practical implications of such a prayer were ever really considered.

Another exception was Adrianus Saravia (c. 1532–1613), a Dutchman who had come to England and become a Canon of Westminster. He became an ardent champion of episcopacy and of historic order in the church. He pointed out that the apostles clearly chose fellow workers and successors to continue their work and that the Lord's promise attached to the missionary mandate at the end of Matthew's gospel, that he would be with the church until the close of the age, must mean that the missionary mandate is to continue until then. It should be noticed, moreover, that the promise is conditional on continuing the work of discipling the nations. Saravia was, however, severely criticized on the continent of Europe for holding such views by both Lutheran and Reformed theologians.

One further observation about the understanding of mission in sixteenth-century England must not be overlooked—the contextualization mandate of Article 34 of the Thirty-Nine Articles (1571). As a Tudor scholar steeped in Greco-Roman oratory,

---

[15]F. E. Brightman, *The English Rite*, vol. 1 (London: Rivington's, 1915), 372–3; Joseph Ketley, *The Two Liturgies . . . of King Edward VI* (Cambridge: Parker Society, 1844), 247. In keeping with his own rejection of antisemitism, Cranmer drew on ancient sources for this collect, but he dropped their reference to the Jews as "deceitful."

Cranmer believed that a message had to be fitted to the cultural particularities of its intended audience. Consequently, in the essay "On Ceremonies" at the end of the first Anglican prayer book (1549), Cranmer established three important principles. First, liturgical practice has not been established by divine revelation but rather by the authority of the church in the light of human culture. Secondly, because society is ever-changing, the church must constantly review its inherited liturgy to make sure that its gospel proclamation remains effective for contemporary culture. It was self-evident to Cranmer that there was no sense in continuing to use deeply hallowed ancient Latin liturgical texts in parochial worship since most English people could not understand them. Thirdly, because human culture differs from nation to nation, all churches will need to contextualize the presentation of the gospel as makes missional sense in their cultural contexts:

And in these all our doings we condemn no other nations, nor prescribe any thing, but to our own people only. For we think it convenient that every country should use such ceremonies, as they shall think best to the setting forth of God's honour and glory, and to the reducing of the people to a most perfect and godly living, without error or superstition; and that they should put away other things, which from time to time they perceive to be most abused, as in men's ordinances it often chanceth diversely in diverse countries.[16]

Cranmer then incorporated these principles in Article 34 of his Forty-Two Articles (1553), which in turn found their final form in Article 34 of the Thirty-Nine Articles (1571):

It is not necessary that Traditions and Ceremonies be in all places one, or utterly like; for at all times they have been diverse, and may be changed according to the diversity of countries, times, and men's manners, so that nothing be ordained against God's word. . . . Every particular or national church hath authority to ordain, change, and abolish ceremonies or rites of the church

---

[16]Ketley, *Two Liturgies*, 155–7.

ordained only by man's authority, so that all things be done to edifying.[17]

Church practices need to be adapted to "men's manners" in different times and places. Even if the Reformation-era Church of England did not actually engage in world mission, its formularies clearly laid down the theological basis for the institutional contextualization of the gospel which has become axiomatic in modern missiology.

The profile of world mission fared a little better in the seventeenth-century revision of the Anglican liturgy. The 1662 *Book of Common Prayer* provides a rite for the "Baptism of such as are of Riper Years," and its preface gives one of the reasons for it as being useful "for the baptizing of Natives in our Plantations and others converted to the faith." And yet, as Stephen Neill points out, there seems to have been only one baptism of an Indian, according to Anglican rites, in the whole of the seventeenth century in spite of there being a British ambassador at the Mughal Court from early in that century, as well as there being chaplains attached to the East India Company. By contrast, already from the middle of the sixteenth century, the Jesuits were making themselves at home at the Mughal Court and in North India generally, making significant contributions to learning, art, and architecture, as well as bringing locals to faith and baptism and planting churches in cities like Lahore and Agra.[18]

Such was the situation, then, until the eighteenth century. There was widespread trust that the liturgical worship of the established church, the homilies and other preaching, and the pastoral offices of "hatching, matching, and dispatching" were sufficient to disciple the nation. As to the rest of the world, there was an uneasy but growing recognition that something should be done about it, but the parochialism of the Reformation era still held sway and not very much was done about it.

During the whole of this period of turmoil, the still significant numbers of those who clung on to the old Catholic faith, had to use all their ingenuity to survive in an atmosphere where, even after Rome had partially relented on pledging loyalty to Elizabeth and

---

[17]Charles Hardwick, *A History of the Articles of Religion* (Cambridge: Deighton Bell, 1859), 318–19 [spelling modernized].
[18]Neill, *History of Christian Missions*, 130, 156, 197–8; John Rooney, *The Hesitant Dawn* (Rawalpindi, Christian Study Centre, 1984), 31–85.

her successors, they were still suspected of treason. Mission was understood as providing for the pastoral and sacramental needs of the faithful. This was dangerous work and many priests and lay people were martyred in the cause of providing for it.[19]

The eighteenth century began quietly enough but it was to prove to be quite as dramatic as the sixteenth, where eventfulness in the church and its mission are concerned.

---

[19]See further, Owen Chadwick, *The Reformation*, 285–93.

2

Learning from the Past

Mission and the Evangelical and Catholic Revivals

How, then, did the morality-based Anglicanism of the seventeenth century change to one so passionately concerned with the proclamation of the gospel of forgiveness and salvation, both overseas and at home? Throughout the seventeenth and for much of the eighteenth century, Anglicanism spread alongside the settlement of English-speaking peoples in different parts of the world. Naturally, as they went, they took their church with them and generally took care that it looked as much like the church at home as was possible. Such settlements needed pastoral care and teaching. These were sometimes provided by "official" chaplains, as with the East India Company, but toward the very end of the seventeenth and the beginning of the eighteenth century, two societies were formed: the Society for Promoting Christian Knowledge (SPCK) and the Society for the Propagation of the Gospel (SPG). The main aim was to "provide the ministrations of the church to British people overseas," but a secondary one was to "evangelize the non-Christian races subject to the crown."[1] In the fulfilling of both aims, the two societies cooperated with the Lutherans in matters

---

[1]Michael Nazir-Ali, *From Everywhere to Everywhere: A World View of Christian Mission* (London: Collins, 1991), 47–8.

like Bible translation and distribution, and in providing pastoral care for settlers, troops, and local converts. Quite remarkably, for high church societies, they found no difficulty in accepting the sacramental and pastoral ministry of German and Danish Lutherans who had not received Episcopal ordination in the Anglican sense.[2]

Such were the early though ambivalent developments in the emergence of missionary awareness among Anglicans. A radical change, however, was to come with the evangelical revival in the Church of England and beyond. The roots of the revival can be traced to an outburst of itinerancy in Wales from around the 1730s. The Welsh were soon joined by George Whitefield and the Wesley brothers, once the latter had gone on from moralism and works-based holiness to a religion of the heart as well as the mind. David Bebbington, historian of the evangelical movement, identifies its leading characteristics as conversionism, activism, biblicism, and crucicentrism. That is to say, bringing people to a living faith in Christ, being active socially and politically, setting great store by the reading and teaching of Scripture, and emphasizing the centrality of Christ's atoning death for us. Each is vitally important in our understanding of evangelicals, but it was the huge energy released for bringing people to faith and to an assurance of forgiveness and of salvation, as long as they remained faithful and showed forth the fruit of faith in good works, which needs to engage our attention. For with religion no longer dominated by moralism and its constant need to prove that a person was good enough for God, the Bible's promise of free pardon released evangelicals from making their own salvation the focus of their piety so that they could turn their attention to the salvation of others.[3]

As a result, we are, once again, drawn back to the peregrinations of the early Scotch-Irish and Anglo-Saxon missionaries. It is the constant movement of the preachers from one town or village to another, from one meeting or congregation to another, from one section of the population to another, that arrests our attention.

---

[2]Stephen Neill, *A History of Christian Missions* (Harmondsworth: Penguin, 1986), 198.
[3]David Bebbington, *Evangelicalism in Modern Britain: A History from the 1730s to the 1980s* (London: Unwin, 1989), 2, 42.

Wesley himself is thought to have preached forty-thousand sermons in the course of his ministry, and huge demands were made on other Methodist ministers as well. They reached out to the gentry as well as to the rural and urban poor, and the concern was always to bring people to Christ and to deepen their faith. Whether such itinerant mission is needed now in an increasingly sedentary church scene is a question being asked today by those who long to see a fresh evangelization in the West.

This energy of the early evangelicals could not be contained within the confines of Great Britain, however many the opportunities there. It spilled over into a concern for the unevangelized in other parts of the world and the duty of Christians to reach them. One of the features of the revival was not to wait for official approval, from the church or state, but to strike out, with like-minded friends, to form societies and prayer groups for the fulfillment of whatever vision God had given those involved in the revival.

One of the catalysts for mission at home and abroad was the newly rediscovered doctrine of means, or the use of human agency by God for the fulfillment of his purposes. The pioneer missionary William Carey (anticipated here by Jonathan Edwards) declared that God uses means for the conversion of the heathen, and we are to ask whether we were those means. The distinct contribution of evangelicals was not the formation of societies. As we have seen, these could be, and were, formed by others. Their distinctive contribution was the introduction of the voluntary principle—that is, the duty of every Christian to be aware of God's calling for them and to respond to this either individually or by joining in with other like-minded people. It is this which led to the proliferation of voluntary societies for the fulfillment of multifarious aims and objects.

The non-denominational London Missionary Society was formed in 1795 for mission overseas, to be closely followed by the Church Missionary Society (CMS) in 1799. The latter was explicitly Anglican (signaled by the word *Church* in its title) but also *voluntary* in that it did not depend on being established as an official body of the church and raised its finances independently from voluntary giving. The formation of the Church Pastoral Aid Society in 1836 for the provision of ordained and lay workers for the church; the Ragged Schools for the poorest; the National Society for elementary education; the movement against slavery; Wilberforce's and Hannah More's project for the "reformation of manners"; the Clapham Sect's and later evangelical campaigns to improve working conditions for men, women, and children; and the revival of nursing as a noble profession (of which Florence Nightingale is a worthy icon), were all either begun by evangelicals or benefitted from their energy. According to Bebbington, although evangelicals were biblically based, they were also deeply influenced by Enlightenment ideas, especially in their view of the human person and his or her relation to the world, particularly in the area of human dignity and equality and in the importance of experience for faith.[4] As I have pointed out elsewhere, it was this evangelical-Enlightenment consensus that created many of the institutions with which we are familiar and which remained in place until it was challenged and eroded, though not destroyed, by the social revolution of the 1960s in the Western world.[5]

Although both SPCK and SPG can be thought of as "high church" societies, the Catholic revival in the Church of England, which followed John Keble's Assize sermon on National Apostasy (1833), also resulted in a fresh awareness of the missionary tasks of the church. At first, as Bishop John D. Davies points out, this revival seems not to have been concerned with missionary issues very much. Its initial *Tracts for the Times* were directed toward the nature of the church and proper obedience to it, but, in the course of time, he claims, the Catholic revival in Anglicanism has made its mark primarily as a missionary movement![6]

We can ask, then, how such a turnaround came to pass and what were its consequences. One catalyst was the desire of many in the movement to serve and worship in churches that were free of the "Erastian taint" of the Church of England. Thus, Hurrell Froude and John Henry Newman were very taken with the romantic idea of being bishops in India without the trammels of the English episcopate. Although there were no offers to them, others like them were to become a feature of the Anglican episcopate in India. The great Bishop Selwyn of New Zealand, although not a missionary

---

[4]Bebbington, *Evangelicalism in Modern Britain*, 50.
[5]Michael Nazir-Ali, *Triple Jeopardy for the West: Aggressive Secularism, Radical Islamism and Multiculturalism* (London: Bloomsbury, 2012), 6.
[6]John D. Davies, *The Faith Abroad* (Oxford: Blackwell, 1983), 1–2.

bishop as such, became a model for the Tractarians of what a bishop should be like. As Bishop Samuel Wilberforce put it, these missionary-type bishops showed the English church that a bishop was "not a sort of embossed ornament to stand at the top of the bannister" but was, rather, necessary to the ordering of the church and fundamental to its missionary task.[7]

The main catalyst, however, was David Livingstone's famous "commerce and Christianity" speech at the Senate House in Cambridge in 1857. The remark has often been misunderstood. Livingstone was arguing for genuine trading relations with Africa rather than falling into the temptation of the lucrative slave trade. As to Christianity, he had long argued that Christians should be prepared to go wherever the slave trader went and to supplant such trade with holistic mission. Livingstone did this himself, as did the early missionaries, even if their advance was often disrupted by Arab slave traders. The speech led, among many other results, to the formation of the Universities' Mission to Central Africa (UMCA). As I have said elsewhere, it is most remarkable that a Scottish Congregationalist should inspire and assist in the founding of an Anglo-Catholic society![8] The society concentrated on missionary bishops planting churches that reflected what Catholic Anglicans thought the "primitive" church was like. There was an emphasis, from the beginning, on prophetic witness against slavery and the slave trade. The building of the Anglican Cathedral in Zanzibar on the very site of the old slave market, with the altar being where the whipping post had been, is an enduring icon of the missionaries' stance against this evil.

The SPG, already "high church," as opposed to the CMS, being merely "church," was also affected by the Catholic revival and, indeed, became one of the main vehicles for Catholic Anglican involvement in world mission. The amalgamation of the two societies—SPG and UMCA to form the United Society for the Propagation of the Gospel (USPG)—in 1965 was an incredibly

---

[7]On this see Peter Williams, *The Ideal of the Self-Governing Church: A Study in Victorian Missionary Strategy* (Leiden: Brill, 1990), 13.

[8]Michael Nazir-Ali, "How the Anglican Communion Began and Where It Is Going," in *Reformation Anglicanism: A Vision for Today's Global Communion*, ed. Ashley Null and John W. Yates III (Wheaton, IL: Crossway, 2017), 30.

significant event in Anglican mission history.[9] John Davies has shown how the commitment to social justice seen in the opposition to slavery was also at work, later on, in Bishop Frank Weston's relentless struggle against forced labor imposed on Africans by the colonial authorities and in the involvement of so many of Anglo-Catholicism's finest missionaries in the long struggle against apartheid. It was, however, Frank Weston himself who, at the Anglo-Catholic Congress of 1923, again drew the attention of his brothers and sisters to poverty in Britain. According to him, worship of Jesus in church should lead us to his presence in the slums of industrial Britain.[10]

This has, indeed, been an Anglo-Catholic commitment from almost the very beginnings of the movement. Talented priests went willingly to work in the poorest parishes. Bryan King at St. George's in the East and Alexander Mackonochie at St. Alban's, Holborn, as well as William Upton Richards of All Saints, Margaret Street, who was, along with Sister Harriet, the founder of the All Saints Sisters of the Poor, one of the first religious orders for women to be founded in the post-Reformation Church of England, readily come to mind. The background was always the terrible poverty in the cities of industrial Britain and the desire of godly parish clergy to find assistance in meeting the needs of the poor. In this connection, Father Peter Mayhew, historian of the All Saints Sisters, tells us that "it was not just that God was calling young women to a life of celibacy, prayer and holiness. He was calling them to a life of charity, to service among the weak and the poor, the aged and the orphaned."[11] Another very good example of such commitment and service, and its mission significance, is the Community of St. John the Divine, an order of nurses and their lay associates, now celebrated in Jennifer Worth's trilogy about her work with them and the television series "Call the Midwife" based on the books which, at its peak, was attaining dizzying ratings! Worth's work has

---

[9]See further Michael Nazir-Ali, *How the Anglican Communion Came To Be and Where It Is Going* (London: Latimer Trust, 2013), 11–12; Neill, *History of Christian Missions*, 265–6; Stephen Neill, *Anglicanism* (Harmondsworth: Penguin, 1960), 342–3.

[10]Davies, *The Faith Abroad*, 28.

[11]Peter Mayhew, *All Saints: Birth and Growth of a Community* (Oxford: All Saints, 1987), 9.

been a witness to Christian love for the poor which reached millions who were probably unreachable in any other way.[12] It seems that the revival of the religious life for both men and women in the Anglican Communion was oriented to service, as well as to prayer and contemplation. The enclosed and contemplative orders came later.

As the religious orders spread to different parts of the world, they took their commitment of working with the poor with them. This involved them in rescuing orphans from destitution, establishing and running schools (both for the poor and for others), nursing in hospitals, and many other kinds of service. Such involvement was not, of course, limited to the orders; many other ordained and laypeople also gave a part, sometimes the whole, of their lives to mission in these ways. Some of their paternalism and attitudes to race may make us uncomfortable today, but there is no doubting the commitment of both evangelical and Catholic Anglican missionaries who sometimes literally took their coffins with them! Our perception, moreover, that they were children of their time should alert us to our own rootedness in our own times and cultures and, if there is a need, to transcend them in the cause of the gospel.

British Roman Catholic involvement in world mission also goes back to the 1822 formation of a branch of the Association for the Propagation of the Faith. The Mill Hill Fathers, the Christian Brothers, and many other religious and lay people have played and continue to play an active role in the worldwide missionary task of the church. Many of these activities and fund raising are now being coordinated by the Pontifical institute known as *Missio*.[13]

---

[12]Jennifer Worth's trilogy is *Call the Midwife* (Orion, London: 2002), *Shadows of the Workhouse* (London: Weidenfeld & Nicolson, 2005), and *Farewell to the East End* (London: Weidenfeld & Nicolson, 2009).

[13]Neill, *Anglicanism*, 335–69; missio.org.uk.

3

Learning Today and Planning for Tomorrow

If we are to plan for the future, we must know about the past; but the present is also extremely important. We have seen how different impulses within the Catholic, Anglican, and wider world led to the emergence and development of a missionary consciousness. Much of what we see around us in global Christianity is a result of this awareness and its practical consequences. We need to ask now about what is happening today, as far as mission and evangelism are concerned. Which churches are growing? Why are they growing? What are their attitudes to the cultures surrounding them, and can the rest of us learn from them?

Missionary Methods

By the time the 1988 Lambeth Conference called for a Decade of Evangelism, many had already been praying about and considering this possibility. Some were, therefore, swift to respond to the call.[1] I remember Joseph Adetiloye, then Bishop of Lagos and later to be Archbishop and Primate of Nigeria, telling me during a pre-Lambeth visit to Nigeria that the Nigerian church was preparing to send missionary bishops to the north of the country as one of its responses to the growing Islamization of Nigeria. This was done promptly

---

[1] *The Truth Shall Make You Free: Report of the Lambeth Conference 1988* (London: Anglican Consultative Council, 1988), 34–5, 231.

after Lambeth and its call for a Decade of Evangelism. In the end, fifteen missionary dioceses were created, and the Church of Nigeria came to be recognized as the fastest growing province of the Anglican Communion.

One of the interesting features of this step is that the Anglican church in Nigeria is a CMS origin church. As we have seen, through much of the nineteenth century, the growing Catholic movement in Anglicanism had been advocating missionary bishops in the sense of pioneers who planted churches that were organized on the lines of the primitive church without the compromises with the state found in the Church of England. This kind of thinking was generally opposed by CMS on the grounds that primary evangelism, church planting, and self-support were needed *before* a church could have bishops. When, in the end, CMS became willing to consider missionary bishops, what it meant was an expatriate missionary serving as bishop of a "native church," on a provisional basis, until a "native" was ready for the episcopate! It is thus revealing that a church, like Nigeria, would appoint missionary bishops very much as pioneer missionaries in the sense advocated earlier by Bishop Wilberforce and the Catholic Anglican societies.[2] As far as we can tell, the strategy of the Nigerian church has been effective in this regard. Those who were a remnant in relatively unchurched parts have gathered around the bishop, and this has led to fresh evangelism and church planting in some of the most challenging situations, often dominated by the kind of Islamist extremism typified by Boko Haram (but not limited to it).

At the other end of Africa, in Kenya, the church has been involved for some time now with the largely nomadic people of northern Kenya. Like the Maasai, the Boran, Gabbra, and Rendille are mobile peoples. They build temporary houses and after pasturing their flocks, herds, and camels in an area for a short time, they move on to fresh pastures and new sources of water. The late Archbishop David Gitari tells us of his work as Bishop of Mt. Kenya East and then Kirinyaga:

---

[2]See John D. Davies, *The Faith Abroad* (Oxford: Blackwell, 1983), 42; and Peter Williams, *The Ideal of the Self-Governing Church: A Study in Victorian Missionary Strategy* (Leiden: Brill, 1990), 14, 52.

The evangelists and even the pastors have to travel with the people when they are ready to move. There can be no permanent church buildings, we must return to the "Tent of Meeting" of the Israelites in the wilderness, soon after the Exodus. Divine Worship, teaching and fellowship have to be structured around the pasturing duties of the tribe.[3]

Likewise, the Catholic missionary Vincent Donovan, in his *Christianity Rediscovered: An Epistle from the Masai*, tells us how the evangelism in a Masai settlement had to take place early in the morning before people went to their shepherding tasks. Those who could not attend because of other duties in the community, were briefed later by those who had been to the pre-breakfast gatherings.[4]

According to Donovan, even the decision to follow Christ and to be baptized was made by the whole Masai community.[5] Gitari, similarly, believes that work among the nomads of northern Kenya should be communitarian, rather than individualistic, in approach. This method of evangelism and discipling is based on the notion of *Ubuntu*, or community solidarity, which characterizes many African societies. John Mbiti, the African theologian, has pointed out that for many Africans, the individual can claim his or her identity only within the context of the community.[6] The obvious danger with such an approach is, of course, the prevention of change if the community is not in favor of it, and it can be asked whether Christianity inevitably produces a heightened consciousness of the person and his or her response to and responsibility before God.[7]

In any case, Gitari goes on to discuss the contextual evangelism which the church has adopted in relation to the nomadic peoples. He relates how the first priest among the *Gabbra* was ordained and, with a camel and forty goats, set about his evangelistic and pastoral

---

[3]David Gitari, "Evangelisation and Culture: Primary Evangelism in Northern Kenya," in *Proclaiming Christ in Christ's Way: Studies in Integral Evangelism*, ed. Vinay Samuel and Albrecht Hauser (Oxford: Regnum, 1989), 101–21.

[4]Vincent J. Donovan, *Christianity Rediscovered: An Epistle from the Masai* (London: SCM Press, 1978), 33.

[5]Donovan, *Christianity Rediscovered*, 75–6.

[6]J. S. Mbiti, *African Religions and Philosophy* (London: Heinemann, 1969), 108–9.

[7]On this, see Larry Siedentop, *Inventing the Individual: The Origins of Western Liberalism* (Harmondsworth: Penguin, 2015).

tasks! This way of equipping pastors and evangelists to adopt the way of life of the nomadic tribes has continued and has led to a number of group conversions. The pastors and evangelists live among the people, travelling in search of water and grazing. It is while travelling or watering the animals that the evangelists share the good news of Jesus Christ with their people. In the evenings, when the community gathers, there can be a discussion about what has been said earlier in the caravan or at the watering hole.[8]

These modern missional examples of planning mission, teaching, and worship in conjunction with the normal rhythms of community life are very much in keeping with the principles of liturgical revision as it is reflected in the sixteenth- and seventeenth-century formularies. Cranmer treasured monastic spirituality's emphasis on praying the Scriptures to inspire love for God in the hearts of worshipers. However, he realized that monasticism's pattern of seven Daily Offices was impossible for most laypeople to follow. Therefore, as part of his commitment to contextualization, Cranmer provided for public worship only two daily morning and evening services in the Church of England, because those were the most convenient times for workers to be able to attend, just as he had noticed that St. Basil the Great had done.[9] We have noted already how provision for adult baptism was made in the 1662 *Book of Common Prayer*, partly to acknowledge a growing sense of missionary needs overseas, even if this was not to begin bearing fruit until the close of the next century. Thus, we see that from the very beginnings liturgical structure sought to follow missional needs, not the reverse.

The work begun by Archbishop Gitari and his team is being continued today by interdenominational bodies like the Eleventh Hour Network, led by Getachew Bezabih, himself an Anglican priest. A number of the nomadic groups have been exposed to Islamization, and the dangers of radicalization are ever present. This makes mission work among them both more challenging and more urgent. A recent consultation between those working with such groups and Christian leaders from the Middle East was very

---

[8]Gitari, "Evangelisation and Culture," 110–21.
[9]Ashley Null, "Divine Allurement: Thomas Cranmer and Tudor Church Growth," in *Towards a Theology of Church Growth*, ed. David Goodhew (Farnham: Ashgate, 2015), 208.

effective in identifying culturally appropriate forms of outreach and also how we can be alert to radicalization, as well as to the steps which need to be taken if it becomes influential in particular communities.

The Anglican Diocese of Karachi in Pakistan, under the leadership of Bishop Chandu Ray, encouraged missionary work both by expatriates from CMS Australia and New Zealand and local workers among the nomadic and semi-nomadic Hindu "untouchables" in the Sind province. The Catholic Church, similarly, through its work with these communities, has brought significant numbers into the Church. Thousands, in fact, have come to faith as a result of the work of different churches and agencies, and the need now is for them to be integrated into the life of churches usually drawn from a very different Punjabi background but also to be able to express their faith, as far as possible, in terms of their own cultural background. Bishop Bashir Jiwan, as the first bishop of the new Diocese of Hyderabad, created in 1980, made evangelism and church planting a priority of his episcopate, but this was, in ways similar to Donovan's and Gitari's, set within the context of a holistic approach to mission. As the mobility of populations increases because of migration and refugees, we will have to learn from such approaches to mission, which are both contextual and "light" in terms of buildings, organizational structures, and mission.[10]

Another area where there has been significant, sometimes explosive, growth is South-East Asia. In Singapore, for example, Christianity grew from being 4 percent of the population in 1900 to around 13 percent today. In Malaysia, it has grown from being 1.5 percent in 1900 to about 9 percent today, with most of the growth being in what used to be the animist interior of Eastern Malaysia and among the ethnically Chinese and Indian communities. Again, in Indonesia, it has increased from 1.4 percent to nearly 14 percent.[11] The Anglican dioceses of Singapore and Sabah have been particularly active in evangelism and church planting. During a visit to the church in Sabah, when I was General Secretary of CMS, I was

---

[10]Gitari, "Evangelisation and Culture," 110–21; *The Truth Shall Make You Free*, 3–4.

[11]D. B. Barrett, G. Kurian, and T. M. Johnson, eds, *World Christian Encyclopedia* (New York: Oxford University Press, 2001), 372, 478, 661.

especially impressed to find single, female Chinese missionaries working deep in the jungles among the *Orang Asli*, or the indigenous inhabitants of the area. This is pioneer mission, indeed, and there can be no doubt that God is blessing such sacrificial service.

Canon Michael Green describes some of the methods used by the churches in this region to grow Christians and to plant churches: The cell group is central to evangelism. Members are committed to bring guests to meetings, and the groups are oriented to welcome and to show hospitality. At some point, when it has grown to a certain number, the cell divides, and the whole task is repeated in the new cells. Cells can also become the basis for a church plant, and these new churches, in turn, generate cell groups and so the story goes on. Unlike traditional home groups in the West, the cell is geared for growth through welcome, teaching, discipleship, and dividing as soon as possible so that more and more cells are created. The church grows wherever and whenever new cells come into existence, people are brought to faith and go out to serve their communities with the love of Christ and to bring more people to Christ.[12]

Nor is this all. A church on fire for mission, like the church in South-East Asia, cannot remain content with mission at home, however successful it may be. It must look also to the world and to cross-cultural mission and evangelism. Here the missionary work of the Anglican Diocese of Singapore deserves notice. Bishop Kuan Kim Seng gives several reasons why the churches in Singapore began to engage in mission outside Singapore. Church leaders were themselves converts and were very aware of the need to fulfill the Great Commission. The charismatic movement inspired people to share the gospel with others. The churches were maturing and had people and financial resources to reach out to the nations in the region. The smallness of Singapore meant that mission energies were not all consumed at home, and churches joined business and other interests in setting up beyond the borders of the city-state.

As far as the Anglican Church is concerned, the Diocese of Singapore began by taking seriously its responsibilities for the nations that were notionally part of its jurisdiction: Cambodia, Indonesia, Laos, Thailand, and Vietnam. Singapore clergy were

---

[12]Michael Green, *Asian Tigers for Christ: The Dynamic Growth of the Church in South East Asia* (London: SPCK, 2001), 43.

appointed deans of these countries, at first, in addition to their own parishes in Singapore itself! They were told not to be content with ministering to expatriates in these countries but to plant indigenous Anglican churches. There are now such churches in Thailand, Cambodia, Indonesia, and Vietnam. Another deanery was created in a country where there was no Anglican church and where Christianity had long been illegal: the nation of Nepal. At the request of local churches and their pastors, who were keen to affiliate with a worldwide fellowship of churches, the Diocese of Singapore, in partnership with Anglican Frontier Missions, agreed to receive these churches and to develop their work and witness to a point where they could become a diocese in their own right. According to Bishop Kuan, this is now set to take place very soon.[13]

Another example of cross-cultural church planting through a diocesan initiative is the way in which the Anglican Diocese of Egypt has provided for the pastoral care of and church planting among Sudanese refugees in Ethiopia. This has now developed into evangelistic and church planting work among other ethnic groups as well. Former Area Bishop Grant LeMarquand's newsletters show that this is a new departure for Anglicans who, in the past, have limited themselves to chaplaincies for expatriates in Ethiopia or working for theological renewal in the Orthodox Tewahedo Church of that country.[14] The presence of Sudanese, Somali, and other ethnic communities has given the church the opportunity to work in this pioneering way without reneging on its commitment to the Ethiopian Orthodox Church.

From Everywhere to Everywhere?

Although the Acts of the Apostles, perhaps for apologetic reasons, presents the missionary movement of the church as being "from Jerusalem to Rome," in fact the gospel, and therefore the church, spread in every direction from the earliest times. Even in Acts, the

---

[13]Kuan Kim Seng, "Southeast Asia and Frontier Missions," in *Shadows from Light Unapproachable: Anglican Frontier Missions (1993–2018)*, ed. Tad Bordenave (Heathsville, VA: Northumberland Historical Press, 2018), 131.

[14]For a sampling of these, see Grant LeMarquand, "Bishop Grant & Doctor Wendy," www.grantandwendy.com.

conversion and baptism of the Queen's high official from Ethiopia (Acts 8:26-39) and the presence of church leaders from Africa in the church at Antioch (Acts 13:1-3) point to an expansion beyond the Greco-Roman world.[15] Outside this world, Armenia and Ethiopia became the first "Christian nations," and Bishop William Young of Pakistan has well documented the expansion of the church in the Persian Empire, the other great superpower of the time, where Christians were tolerated and persecuted in turn.[16] The Church of the East, as this church likes to be called, has had a glorious mission history of evangelization and the planting of churches in Central Asia, India, and China, both before and after the rise of Islam in this region.[17]

Even during the modern missionary movement when mission was seen as being "from the West to the rest," the actual carriers of the good news were often indigenous Christians who took the faith to their own people or to others in their vicinity. The Reverend Abdul Masih, who was a Muslim convert and the first Anglican priest in India, was engaged in a pioneer ministry in Agra after his baptism in 1811. He combined evangelism with traditional Unani (Hellenistic medicine) and had established a church in Agra *before* expatriate CMS missionaries arrived in the area. Toward the end of the nineteenth century, the Mozambican martyr Bernard Mizeki helped in the opening up of the country now known as Zimbabwe to Christian mission. Apolo Kivebulaya of Uganda took the faith to the Congo and, of course, Bishop Adjai Crowther led the mission on the Niger River which opened up Nigeria to the gospel. In East Africa also, the gospel was often spread by the first converts who took it to the hinterland and expressed it in ways more suited to the cultures of the people among whom they found themselves.[18]

---

[15]See I. Howard Marshall, *The Acts of the Apostles* (Grand Rapids, MI: Eerdmans, 1984), 17; Henry Chadwick, *The Early Church*, revised edition (Harmondsworth: Penguin, 1993), 9.

[16]William G. Young, *Patriarch, Shah and Caliph* (Rawalpindi: Christian Study Centre, 1974).

[17]E. A. Wallis Budge, *The Monks of Kublai Khan* (London: Religious Tract Society, 1928), 13.

[18]On all of this, see Jocelyn Murray, *Proclaim the Good News: A Short History of the Church Missionary Society* (London: Hodder, 1985), 27, 127, 250; Margaret Snell, *Bernard Mizeki of Zimbabwe* (Harare: Mambo Press, 1986); Williams, *Ideal of the Self-Governing Church*, 11; and Michael Nazir-Ali, *From Everywhere to Everywhere: A World View of Christian Mission* (London: Collins, 1991), 208.

Today, we are in a situation where a clear and growing majority of Christians is to be found in Asia, Africa, and Latin America. How should this affect our thinking about global mission generally and evangelism and church planting in particular? At the same time, while churches in the West are still relatively wealthy, their human resources (especially, but not only, in terms of cross-cultural mission) are much more slender. The missionary challenge in the West is also becoming much more significant. What gifts of people, talent, and money has the Lord of the church given to his church so that it may fulfill the Great Commission he has left for it?

Just recently, I was invited to a gathering in Argentina about the persecuted church in the Middle East, China, and Africa. It was heart-warming to meet Christians from Latin America working in some of the most restricted situations in the world. We also heard from Christians who were working within their own regions, and we met those who have been tortured and imprisoned for their faith—the living martyrs of our day. Argentinians are able to send out "tent makers" for mission to countries that may be quite closed to any Western initiatives. This is also true of South Koreans and Indians. The Chinese have re-entered the field with the "Back to Jerusalem" movement, which aims to evangelize and to plant churches among people between China and Jerusalem. That gives the movement some scope!

The West is also rapidly becoming a large mission field. This is not only because of immigration and refugees, although that is a significant factor in many countries, but also because of the loss of faith among so many. Christians and churches in the West have to learn again the arts of evangelism, apologetics, and church planting but they should engage in this mission in partnership with those from other parts of the world. At a Chinese Christian Fellowship celebration of the Chinese New Year in an English city, I was particularly impressed with the way in which Christian faith was expressed, quite naturally, in Chinese idiom, but it was its freshness that made its impact on many secular folk who would not otherwise darken the door of a church. The vibrancy of music and creativity in the Afro-Caribbean-led churches, the hospitality of the Asian ones, and the directness of the Americans can all contribute to making Christian faith credible again in the West.

It was for reasons such as these that, more than thirty years ago, I wrote my book *From Everywhere to Everywhere: A World View of Christian Mission.* Mission cannot any longer be confined to "sending" and "receiving" countries. Denominations, mission agencies, and parachurch groups have to put together resources of people, money, and training and apply them to the neediest situations without regard to where each resource has come from. This is harder than it might appear, as churches want to "own" missionaries and their work. They want their own people to go out and wish to support them when they do. This may be natural and even laudable but it will need to be set aside for greater effectiveness in the task of fulfilling the Great Commission, whether on "the doorstep" or in lands far away.

If "from Jerusalem to Rome" was the first phase of mission and the "Nestorian" mission to Asia important for our understanding of the church's potential for universal mission, the last episode of mission "from the West" has sown the seeds of a truly global fellowship of churches and Christians. We are now on the threshold of mission "from everywhere to everywhere." What aspects of it should we keep in mind as we enter this new age? Are the people in our pews ready to respond to God calling? How should we be equipping them to be evangelists and church planters? It is to these questions that we now turn.

Many years ago, I outlined a "mission grid" which would allow us to audit our mission thinking and activities. In God's providence, the grid is being used by researchers to explore what mission means in specific contexts and how churches are planning and delivering their mission strategies of one kind or another. I am hoping now to use a modified version of this grid to set out how I think we should be engaging in authentic mission during the twenty-first century.

4

Incarnational Presence?

Ecclesia Anglicana has traditionally identified with the church being the body of Christ in a particular place. Even Thomas Cranmer can be shown to relate this to the celebration of the Eucharist in every parish:

> All faithful Christians [be] spiritually turned into the body of Christ, and so be joined unto Christ, and also together among themselves, that they do make but one mystical body of Christ, as St Paul saith: "We be one bread and one body, as many as be partakers of one bread and one cup."[1]

In many liturgies today, we say that we "share in the body of Christ" and that the Eucharist makes us "one body." Scripture certainly provides a warrant for this kind of language: partaking of the body of Christ in the Eucharist makes us one body (1 Cor. 10:17). In addition, just a little later, Paul also describes us as being different parts of the body of Christ (1 Cor. 12:12-27), and in the letters to the Ephesians and Colossians, he goes on to speak of Christ as the head of his body, the church (Eph. 1:22-23; 4:15-16; Col. 1:18, etc.). During Paul's conversion experience, the Lord identified himself with his people, saying, "Saul, Saul, why do you persecute *me*?" (Acts 9:4; 22:7; 26:14 NIV). It has long been suggested that this event was fateful, for Paul, in his identification of the church as the body of Christ. Along with these verses, Paul's strongly

---

[1] J. E. Cox, *Writings and Disputations of Thomas Cranmer ... Relative to the Sacrament of the Lord's Supper* (Cambridge: Parker Society, 1844), 42.

incorporationist language about baptism (Rom. 6:3-11) and his sense of the church partaking of the body and blood of the Lord lead to the ubiquitous "*en Christo*" formula: everything in the Christian life flows from being in Christ and Christ being in us (*Christos en hemin*). Cranmer also enshrined this biblical principle in the Anglican liturgy as the purpose of Holy Communion: "that we may evermore dwell in him, and he in us."[2]

It is this background which has led those of Anglican heritage to think of the church in incarnational terms in relation to its presence and work in villages, towns, and even nations: the church, as the body of Christ, should seek to be present in every human community so that it may bear witness to its head and Savior. Indeed, such an approach has even been described as "the religion of the incarnation." The parochial system, as it developed in England and has since spread worldwide, is an example of such incarnationalist thinking. It seeks to divide up the country geographically so that there is a church for every single community in the land. At any rate, such is the theory. This approach has its strengths in terms of a committed presence, through good times and bad, in every community where there is opportunity to be present. When the system works well, it can be an effective channel of communicating the gospel.[3]

Nevertheless, as we shall see, such a view of the church's nature and work has been criticized as claiming too much for itself and as identifying itself with Christ in a way that puts it beyond challenge and reform. It has also been claimed that too closely identifying the institutional church with the risen Lord Jesus sanctifies the status quo, and may build on old paganisms rather than witnessing to Christ's uniqueness over and against those holding on to ancient idols. For these and other reasons, other models of the church have been brought forward. Anglican formularies attempt to maintain a balance between the church as of divine origin (e.g., the *Ordinal*

---

[2]See John A. T. Robinson, *The Body: A Study in Pauline Theology* (London: SCM, 1952), 46, 68 and passim. Cf. C. F. D. Moule, *The Origin of Christology* (Cambridge: Cambridge University Press, 1990), 69; and Joseph Ketley, *The Two Liturgies . . . of King Edward VI* (Cambridge: Parker Society, 1844), 279.

[3]Charles Gore, ed., *Lux Mundi: A Series of Studies in the Religion of the Incarnation* (London: John Murray, 1889). The book's influence is celebrated in Robert Morgan, ed., *The Religion of the Incarnation: Essays in Commemoration of Lux Mundi* (Bristol: Bristol Classical Press, 1989).

frequently speaks of the church of God and, in prayer, speaks of "thy church") and as a human institution, albeit with a divine vocation through Christ. Although God works through its preaching and sacraments to bring people to a saving faith and living relationship with him, church leaders can and do make mistakes, and not just in failing to practice at all times biblical morality, but even failing always to uphold biblical truth (Articles 19, 20, and 26). Later on, we will examine other ways of understanding the church, but, in the meanwhile, and taking the above strictures into account, we shall consider what incarnational presence can mean.

The Parish and Presence

Going back to the very roots after its early missionary origins, Theodore of Tarsus (602–90), the great reforming Archbishop of Canterbury, organized the English church in a form which we can still recognize today. On his arrival, at the ripe old age of sixty-six, he set about visiting the whole of the church in England, filling vacant sees and creating new ones. By summoning synods, he set a pattern for corporate decision-making. Along with his companion, Hadrian the African, he also established an educational system for the country. In addition to all of this, he did a great deal to create the now-familiar parochial system for England. Much of what we recognize as typically *Ecclesia Anglicana* (i.e., the parish, the school, synodal decision-making, etc.) was brought to England by these two men of God, one Asian and the other African!

However, as Bishop John Moorman has pointed out, the origins of the parochial system also lie in the feudal system. The parish church was usually on manorial land, and the priest was chosen by the local thegn, although licensed and instituted by the bishop. The priest's income derived from the people in the parish. Moreover, given Gregory the Great's instruction to St. Augustine of Canterbury not to destroy the pagan temples and shrines of the pagan English but to purify them and use them for Christian worship, it is likely that many parish churches were, and are, on pre-Christian "sacred space." Thus, while the parish system came to cover the whole land and became also the basic unit of civil administration, this kind of "presence" is always in danger of compromise with the wider community with which it is so closely integrated. Cranmer and his fellow Reformers looked to the English monarch as the only one in the land powerful enough to make the reform of the church, and its purging of what they saw as medieval accretions, possible. However, the incipient dangers of Erastianism, later to bear much fruit, have been so ably identified by Philip Turner and Ephraim Radner. They warn that state-sponsored/state-regulated religion does not merely lead to the "High Establishment" of the appointment of bishops, as political rather than religious figures, and the presence of some of them in the legislature, etc., but its compromises with establishment culture are woven into the life of the church at every level.[4] In fairness, it has to be pointed out that many of these features—for example, the state's role in the appointment of bishops and their founding role in the House of Lords—predate the Henrician Reformation. In spite of these dangers, the parish system has been a basic way of expressing Christian presence in a locality. Even where the situation in England cannot be replicated, as in the United States or South Asia, the values of relating to the wider community, inviting the community in, and going out in service to it often characterize effective presence.

Sometimes presence may seem anachronistic. This is so, for example, in contexts where another faith tradition is dominant. An instance that readily comes to mind is that of the Anglican chaplaincies in the Arabian/Persian Gulf. Most were established when these small sheikhdoms were British protectorates mainly for expatriate British officials, workers, and soldiers. After the exponential rises in the price of petroleum and related products, however, these countries became increasingly wealthy and important for the global economy. Some of them, like the United Arab Emirates and Qatar, are actively seeking to diversify their economies away from excessive dependence on oil. Such a heady mix of factors has led to large numbers of people from the Arab world, South Asia, the Philippines, every part of Africa, and, of course, from the Western world to come and work in these states. Many of these workers are Christians ranging from Latin and Eastern rite Catholics and

---

[4]See further Bede, *The Ecclesiastical History of the English People* (Oxford: Oxford University Press, 2008), 1:30, 56–7; J. R. H. Moorman, *A History of the Church in England*, 3rd edition (London: A&C Black, 1976), 23; and Ephraim Radner and Philip Turner, *The Fate of Communion* (Grand Rapids, MI: Eerdmans, 2006).

Orthodox to Protestants and Pentecostals of every description. The Catholic, Orthodox, and Anglican chaplaincies, often being the only authorized church buildings in a city or town, became focal points for the spiritual life of many of these communities. The hospitality offered by these chaplaincies has been generous, and numerous ecclesial bodies have benefitted from it. Chaplaincy life and worship, similarly, has changed from being predominantly European to a rich mix of Asian, African, and everything else!

The ethnicity of the clergy, in the Anglican chaplaincies, for example, has been slower in changing, but that is also happening to some extent. This has not been so for diocesan structures, which have continued to be "English" in both ethos and personnel. One reason that is sometimes given for this is the presence of British sovereign bases in Cyprus and the need for ministry there. Another reason that is given is that the ruling families in the Gulf regard the Anglican Church as "the Queen's Church" and it is necessary, therefore, that the senior clergy should be English or, at least, European. To an outsider, this may seem like especial pleading, particularly when the situation, and people's perceptions with it, are changing so fast. Be that as it may, it is certainly true that the mere presence of these chaplaincies, anachronistic as they may have seemed, made a pastoral and missionary response possible in very challenging circumstances.[5]

Mention of this "newer" presence in Islamic contexts reminds us, of course, of the continued and continuing presence of the ancient churches there, whether Chalcedonian Orthodox, Oriental Orthodox, Uniate Catholic, or Assyrian. They have struggled over the centuries to maintain a presence under the often crippling conditions of the *Dhimma* (the highly restrictive provisions under which certain kinds of non-Muslims were allowed to remain in Islamic domains). Even where churches could be retained, they could be repaired only with hard-to-obtain permission. New ones could not be built, and no Christian symbolism, such as crosses, could be displayed in public, and the sound of church bells was forbidden. There could be no open preaching of the gospel, and apostasy from Islam, even of previously converted Christians, was punishable with death.

---

[5]On this see, Michael Nazir-Ali, *From Everywhere to Everywhere: A World View of Christian Mission* (London: Collins, 1991), 60–1, 144.

As with their doctrinal opposites, the Assyrians, the Copts also have had a significant mission history outside the Islamic world, in Nubia, Sudan, Ethiopia, and Eritrea. Within that world, however, when they have not been subject to persecution, the most they have been able to do is to celebrate the Divine Liturgy and to bring up their children in the faith, hoping that this will not be eroded by the many attractions of conversion, especially for women, through marriage. It is wonderful to see today how these churches are renewing their sense of mission: this is seen in a revival of the monastic vocation, particularly among professionals, in the public teaching of the faith by bishops and priests, with many from non-Christian backgrounds attending and benefiting from such teaching, and in fresh interest in church-planting, for example, in sub-Saharan Africa.[6] Critical to the future of mission within Islamic contexts is the question of religious freedom and adherence to the Universal Declaration on Human Rights to which most states are signatories, in particular Article 18 of this declaration on freedom of religion and belief. The substance and intention of this Article seems to be missing from equivalent declarations emanating from the Islamic world.[7] We have to ask why and what the implications of this are for the future of a Christian presence in the Islamic world.

Behind the Iron Curtain, too, Christian life was severely restricted. When the Russian Orthodox Patriarch was asked, in those days, to describe his church, he said, "It is a church that celebrates the Divine Liturgy." That is, more or less, all that it was allowed to do! It was not permitted any activity outside church buildings; the children of believers could not be catechized, and the church was not able to serve the wider community in any way. Those who defied the Communist government faced exile, imprisonment, or hard labor in "re-education" camps. Even mere presence, however, encouraged many and brought some to question and even to reject atheistic Marxism. Since the disappearance of the Iron Curtain, churches have often experienced significant growth and renewal,

---

[6]For example, see Iris Masry, *Introduction to the Coptic Church* (Cairo: Dar El Alam, 1977); Maurice Assad, "Mission in the Coptic Church: Perspective, Doctrine and Practice in Mission Studies," in Mission Studies 4, no. 1 (1987): 21–34.

[7]On this see Michael Nazir-Ali, *Faith, Freedom and the Future: Challenges for the Twenty-First Century* (London: Wilberforce Publications, 2016), 98, 156–7.

but much of this is due to the hard graft of survival during the dark years.[8]

Preaching Orders and Presence

From an early period, monasticism has presented a particular way of being present. In late antiquity, it was a witness to an increasingly lax society and church, calling people back to evangelical simplicity and holiness. In the Islamic world, the presence of monks is noted as being of one of humility (Qur'an 5:85) and of prayer and devotion (Q3:113–14). The great Pakistani philosopher and statesman Allama Iqbal points out that the living example of the monks was one of the triggers for the rise of Sufism or Islamic mysticism. He claims that it was the actual life of the hermits and monks, rather than their religious ideas, which fascinated the early Sufis, even if lifestyle and belief cannot be easily separated.[9] It has often been pointed out that the Benedictine movement made possible the survival of learning, moral development, and civility during the Dark Ages in Europe. As another dark age approaches, Alasdair MacIntyre goes on to argue for the so-called Benedict option—that is, the emergence of local communities where spiritual, moral, and intellectual life cannot only survive but even flourish and from which the surrounding culture can be renewed.[10]

As far as mission-mindedness is concerned, however, it was the emergence in the late Middle Ages of the preaching orders or the friars; the most significant of these were the Dominicans and the Franciscans. The emphasis of the former was on preaching the truth and refuting error. From the beginning, they invested a great deal in education. The Franciscans, while certainly not averse to learning, emphasized the imitation of Christ in poverty, humility, and suffering. Their preaching up and down England (as an example) transformed the country. In an age when the parish clergy were, by

---

[8]Nazir-Ali, *From Everywhere to Everywhere*, 140–1.

[9]Muhammad Iqbal, *The Development of Metaphysics in Persia* (Lahore: Bazm-i-Iqbal, 1964), 80.

[10]Alasdair MacIntyre, *After Virtue: A Study in Moral Theory* (London: Duckworth, 2000), 263.

and large, not given to preaching, the vigorous sermons of the friars were warmly welcomed by the populace, which had been starved of hearing the word of God. It is true that as the friars became increasingly wealthy through the patronage of the rich and powerful and the alms of ordinary people, they became more lax and subsequently attracted the ire of would-be reformers like John Wycliffe.[11]

It was St. Francis of Assisi's own interest in mission among Muslims that led him to enunciate his First Rule, a set of statutes for the emerging order (1221). In its chapter 16, he famously sets out the two modes of mission which the friars and their lay companions were to adopt: the first is that of mere presence. They were to go into the Muslim and other worlds, declaring themselves to be Christians and submitting to every human authority. When they discerned that it was God's will, they should then proclaim the word of God and invite people to believe and be baptized. It should be noted that the instruction was to positively preach the gospel without specifically criticizing other religions or systems of belief. The briefer Second Rule (1223), at the behest of the pope, emphasized the witness of life but said nothing about avoiding disputes and little about the right time for preaching the gospel. This is interesting because many Franciscans, in their missionary work, emphasized explicit preaching and often denounced another religion. This led to many martyrdoms, and some even sought such a death. It seems that they were listened to with sympathy as long as they preached about Jesus, but their hearers turned against them when the friars began to criticize their religion.[12]

In more recent times, some Franciscans have gone back to the teaching of the First Rule about presence. They have established themselves on housing estates and urban communities, seeking to minister to people's needs, such as education for their children, a place for meditation and contemplation, and the offer of friendship. In all of this, it is through the witness of life that they seek to commend the gospel. Anglican Franciscans, where they exist and

---

[11]Moorman, *History of the Church in England*, 102.
[12]For a detailed discussion, see Jean-Marie Gaudeul, *Encounters and Clashes: Islam and Christianity in History*, vol. 1 (Rome: Pontifical Institute for the Study of Arabic and Islamic Studies, 1984), 151.

where circumstances permit, do lead missions which actively seek to bring people to Christ.[13]

Life Witness and Buildings

One of the questions is whether the witness of life prepares people for the preaching of the gospel. Charles de Foucauld (1858–1916), who was called to live and work in the remote regions of Algeria, among the Tuareg, won the universal admiration of both the French colonial power and the Berbers for his life of prayer and of charitable work, although there were no converts as a result of his ministry. He planned for communities of "Little Brothers" and "Little Sisters" to join him, but none did. It was only after his death that such communities began to emerge and are now to be found in the poorest and most unsettled parts of the world. We can also ask whether the movements toward Christ among the Berber populations of North Africa, mainly of an evangelical flavor, nevertheless, owe something to the sacrificial life of witness of people like De Foucauld. What then will be the harvest of the witness of life of "the Little Brothers" and "the Little Sisters of Jesus" in countries like Iran and Pakistan, where they live in situations of danger, marginalization, and persecution?

In terms of a contemporary understanding of mission, an important question is posed by St. Francis' First Rule: What is the right balance between the use of resources for an effective presence (this includes the maintenance of physical structures but is not limited to it), the continuing task of discerning appropriate ways of proclamation, and the allocation of proper resources both for the process of discernment and the proclamation itself?

St. George's Church in Baghdad, although founded by missionaries from Jerusalem, became a typical Anglican "chaplaincy" church for expatriates. It was closed by Saddam Hussein after the Iraqi invasion of Kuwait, which led to the First Gulf War. The church was looted and lying derelict when Andrew White, who came to be known as the Vicar of Baghdad, started to take services there. The church began to grow exponentially, although for security reasons it had to

---

[13]Nazir-Ali, *From Everywhere to Everywhere*, 143.

be moved away temporarily from the building itself. When I visited it, some years later, it was back in action! Situated in the "Red Zone," where all the violence was and gunfire could be heard in the grounds, it was an oasis where people came to pray, to be fed, and to be seen by doctors, nurses, and dentists. They came to be prayed for and healed. They came from every religious background, and there was hospitality and help for all of them. This ministry continues under Andrew's successor, Father Fa'iz Jirjis, and is a dramatic model of how to keep presence and outreach aligned.[14]

It was Andrew who took me to see the *Dar al-Mahabba*, or House of Love, run by Mother Teresa's Sisters, mainly from India and Bangladesh. They are bringing up abandoned children who have severe disabilities, many of them caused, directly or indirectly, by Saddam Hussain's chemical and biological attacks on his own people. They are being brought up as Christians, with prayer, Bible reading, and the singing of choruses. When I asked whether anyone objected, the sisters replied that no one else wanted these children anyway, so who would object? Their house was the only one without any security, standing without walls in the street. Again, when I expressed concern about this, the sisters laughed and said that they were the only good thing happening in that area and no one would touch them. A wonderful example of holding together presence, service, and mission, and of making the marginalized the center of our missionary concern!

One question that is often raised is the importance of buildings. I remember being shown around a city in northern Nigeria and remarking that it must be a Muslim majority city since there were prominent mosques on every important junction. My hosts tried to dispel this perception and told me that the city was evenly divided between Muslims and Christians. To which I replied, "But where are the churches?" It is true that there were churches, but they were down the streets and in the suburbs—you wouldn't know they were there unless someone took you there!

In cultures where people are used to public places of worship, which symbolize presence, it is most important for Christian communities to have a physical presence which can reflect a spiritual

---

[14]Andrew White, *The Vicar of Baghdad* (Oxford: Monarch, 2009), 143; and White, *My Journey So Far* (Oxford: Lion, 2015), 153.

presence. Of course, the church is God's people, and the early church did not possess buildings as such. They worshiped in the upper rooms of wealthy benefactors in Asia and in homes in Rome (sometimes donated for this purpose). They went to the synagogue as long as they were allowed to do so, and prayed at the tombs of the martyrs, but when it became possible for them to do so, from the third century or so, they began to build dedicated places of worship because they saw the importance of such a place for teaching, prayer, and worship.[15] As T. S. Eliot says in his poem *Little Gidding*, "You are here to kneel / Where prayer has been valid."[16]

Islamic law has a surer sense of this importance in its restrictions on places of worship for Jews and Christians. Popular Muslim sentiment also makes it very difficult for churches to be built and used for worship. This is why the maintenance, repair, and building of church buildings remains a critical issue in Muslim–Christian relations from Egypt to Indonesia. Buildings have to do with identity, community, and a sense of security in pressurized situations. It is necessary, therefore, for denominations, mission agencies, charitable trusts, and so on to take seriously the need for a physical presence in contexts such as the Islamic world and not to insist, for example, on finance only for "people-related work." We must make sure, however, that such buildings are appropriate for the work that needs doing and do not appear alien in the cultural context.[17]

---

[15]See the report by the Interfaith Consultative Group, *Communities and Buildings: Church of England Premises and Other Faiths* (London: Church House Publishing, 1996).

[16]T. S. Eliot, *Little Gidding*, in *Four Quartets* (New York: Harcourt, 1943), 1:45-46.

[17]Michael Nazir-Ali, *Frontiers in Muslim-Christian Encounter* (Oxford: Regnum, 1987), 77.

5

Going Walkabout

Peregrination and Mission

If speaking of the church as the body of Christ leads to an incarnational view of the church that is centered on place and community, another model might be to speak of the pilgrim people of God, journeying to their heavenly home and the kingdom of God.

Such language is no less rooted in the Bible: for example, in the story of the Exodus, in Jesus's own largely itinerant ministry, and in the missionary journeys of the first apostolic bands. In the first letter of Peter, we find Christians described as aliens and exiles in this world, with the implication that we should not become so rooted in the present order that we lose sight of the world and the life to come (1 Pet. 1:1; 2:11-12).

We saw earlier that there was a contrast between the Celtic emphasis from the north on itinerant missionaries in the evangelization of England and the inclination toward the establishing of diocesan and parish structures in the missionaries from the south and east. This difference in emphasis should not be overdrawn. The Celts also founded important centers for missionary and pastoral activity (such as Iona or Lindisfarne), and the Roman missionaries were also itinerant in reaching many parts of England.

The tension, however, between itinerancy and the mission station approach has remained. Those of 'Anglican' tradition, if they have thought about local mission at all, have tended to see the parish church as a center for such mission. What happens then to the itinerant missionary who goes from place to place to bring the gospel to the people? What about bands of such missionaries and programs for such mission? What, if anything, can we say about them?

Even if we don't buy the exaggerated picture of the ministry of Jesus in Pier Paolo Pasolini's famous film *The Gospel According to Matthew*, it is clear that this ministry, as portrayed in the Gospels, was itinerant:

> Jesus went about all Galilee, teaching in their synagogues and healing every disease and every infirmity among the people. So his fame spread throughout all Syria, and they brought all the sick, those afflicted with various diseases and pains, demoniacs, epileptics and paralytics, and he healed them. And great crowds followed him from Galilee and the Decapolis and Jerusalem and Judaea and from beyond the Jordan.
>
> Matt. 4:23-25

This passage neatly sums up the essential mobility of Jesus's teaching and work. The itinerancy was complemented by being at home, retiring (alone or with his disciples) to pray, and setting his face toward Jerusalem (Mark 2:1; 3:9; 6:30-32; 9:28; Luke 9:51; etc.).

Not only was Jesus itinerant himself but in his sending of the twelve and then the seventy (or seventy-two), we see that he equipped others to be travelling missionaries as well (Matt. 10:5; 28:18-20; Mark 6:7; Luke 9:1; 10:1; John 17:18; etc.). We should not be surprised, then, that in fulfilling the Great Commission, the early disciples were also itinerant: the scattering of the church because of persecution displaced many to different parts of Palestine and beyond (Acts 8:4). As they traveled, they proclaimed the word wherever they went, even as far as Antioch, where the disciples were first called Christians and from where the mission to the nations can be said to have begun (Acts 11:19). Paul's great missionary journeys, of course, began from Antioch, and he and his fellow missionaries were commissioned by the church there (Acts 13:1f).

Alongside this itinerant element, we have to note with Roland Allen that these apostolic missionaries were quick to establish local churches and to provide a ministry of governance, teaching, and leadership (Acts 14:23; 20:17-18; Rom. 16:1-2; 1 Cor. 12:28-29; Eph. 4:11-12; 1 Tim. 5:17-18; 2 Tim. 1:6; etc.). They did not prolong their own presence unnecessarily because they believed that God would provide each local church with the ministry it needed.[1] The tension, as we saw earlier, between the CMS ideal of a local church, which would produce its own ministry, and the missionary bishop, who goes out to plant a church and then to lead it, remains and is, perhaps, inherent in the continuing missionary task of the church.

Charles Gore, in his critical work *The Ministry of the Christian Church*, points out that almost from the very beginning there has been a settled ministry in the local church of presbyter-bishops and deacons and a wider, itinerant ministry of "prophets" and "apostles." He cites the early (most likely first century) *Didache*, or *The Teaching of the Twelve Apostles*, which recognizes this distinction. His purpose, of course, in noticing these ministries is to argue that the emergence of the office of a bishop is not just one from among the presbyters becoming their presiding officer but also in succession to these apostolic figures who exercised ministries of teaching, preaching, encouragement, and oversight as they traveled around the local churches. He points out that already in the figures of James in Jerusalem and of Timothy and Titus, such a ministry of oversight was becoming localized. The *Didache* explicitly makes provision for such localization. According to Gore, the office of bishop draws not only on the pastoral tasks of the presbyters but on the apostolic functions of these itinerant figures. Whatever may have been the importance of these figures in the emergence of the episcopate, in terms of our discussion, it seems clear that in the early church the settled and the itinerant ministries were complementary.[2]

Missionary Activism

We have seen how the emergence of the preaching orders in the later Middle Ages renewed the work of itinerant preaching, both to strengthen the faith of believers and to proclaim the gospel to non-Christians. John Wycliffe and Lollardy, only a little later, produced the "Poor Preachers" who went about the countryside preaching

---

[1]Roland Allen, *Missionary Methods: St. Paul's or Ours? A Study of the Church in the Four Provinces* (Cambridge: Lutterworth, 2006).
[2]Charles Gore, *The Ministry of the Christian Church* (London: Rivington's, 1889), 271; Aaron Milavec, ed., *The Didache* (Collegeville, MN: Liturgical Press, 2003), 11:3-4, 13:1-2.

the gospel and denouncing the corruption in the church wherever they found it. Some of them were recruited into the Great Revolt of 1381, which resulted in the horrific murder of the Archbishop of Canterbury, but many were genuine precursors of the Reformation, especially in their adherence to the doctrine of *Sola Scriptura*, as they understood it.[3]

The evangelical revival of the eighteenth century onward was rooted in the itinerant preaching of George Whitefield and John Wesley. Wesley was indefatigable in his itinerancy: he traveled several thousand miles annually on horseback. It is estimated that during his fifty-two years of active ministry, he covered some two hundred and twenty-five thousand miles, preached some forty thousand sermons, and published around four hundred books and pamphlets! Nor was he alone in this. A working week of ninety to one hundred hours was expected of Methodist preachers. An energetic ministry of visiting peoples in their homes, weekday Bible study, and preaching were also characteristic of evangelical clergy in the established church. While some endorsed Wesleyan itinerancy, others, like Charles Simeon, found they had enough to do in their parish.[4]

In the English-speaking world, the evangelicals were, of course, pioneers in world mission, and although much of mission, in different parts of the world, was based at mission stations, a great deal, of necessity, was itinerant. A good example of this is the three Niger expeditions organized and supported by CMS, the British colonial authorities, and traders in the middle years of the nineteenth century. In retrospect, it may have been better for Christian mission for CMS not to have become involved with the traders and the authorities, but the missionaries were dependent on the others for transport and supplies. Contact was, therefore, unavoidable. Samuel Adjai Crowther participated in all three expeditions. Later to be Anglican bishop on the Niger, Crowther was a Yoruba freed slave who had been ordained in Sierra Leone. In fact, the work of evangelism and church planting in what came to be called the Niger

---

[3]J. R. H. Moorman, *A History of the Church in England*, 3rd edition (London: A&C Black, 1976), 118.
[4]David Bebbington, *Evangelicalism in Modern Britain: A History from the 1730s to the 1980s* (London: Unwin, 1989), 10; Moorman, *History of the Church in England*, 297.

Mission was often carried out by clergy and catechists from Sierra Leone and, later, from Yoruba land itself, because the rate of mortality for Europeans was very high in the early years. There was also constant internecine warfare in the area and resistance to a European presence made mission by Africans and for Africans necessary as well as desirable.[5]

Another story from later in the nineteenth century is that of Thomas Valpy French (1825–91), a CMS missionary and educationalist who was one of the founders of St. John's College, Agra, and who went on to become the first Anglican bishop of Lahore in what is today Pakistan. Having resigned his see, he became the first missionary in Oman and was engaged in a most demanding itinerant mission, in the heat of the Omani summer, when he died of exhaustion. In the whole of his life, he was ready to go wherever the Lord called him to go.[6]

Someone who could not easily fit into the framework of Anglican theological training was a young Sikh convert, Sundar Singh (1889–1929). After expressing initial hostility to the Christian faith, he was dramatically converted, and having tried training for a pastoral ministry, he set out to become a Christian *sadhu* in the style of Indian "holy men" who wander from place to place, bringing their message to any willing to hear them. His work up and down the South Asian subcontinent enabled people to see the faith in genuine Indian garb. He traveled extensively in the West as well and was well received by people in Europe, the United States, and Australia. This tradition of Christian *sadhus* has continued, and although it can be abused, it has been an effective form of itinerant ministry in India and beyond.[7]

In our own times, too, evangelism has often been characterized by itinerant preachers who have taken advantage of modern communications to traverse the world with the message of salvation. Billy Graham, who tirelessly traveled to different parts of the world for many decades, springs immediately to mind. So many Christians

[5]Jocelyn Murray, *Proclaim the Good News: A Short History of the Church Missionary Society* (London: Hodder, 1985), 50.

[6]Vivienne Stacey, *Thomas Valpy French, First Bishop of Lahore* (Lahore: Masihi Isha'at Khana, 1979), 120.

[7]A. J. Appasamy, *Sundar Singh: A Biography* (Madras: Christian Literature Society, 1976).

today, not to mention church leaders, owe their coming to faith, at least in human terms, to Billy Graham's missions.[8] What Graham was doing all over the world, the irrepressible duo Michael Cassidy and Bishop Festo Kivengere were doing in Africa through their organization African Enterprise. They have tried to bring the gospel, with all its promise and demand, to deeply divided and conflicted situations in South Africa (Michael Cassidy's home) and Uganda (Festo Kivengere's home). Not only have they brought people to personal faith in Christ through numerous evangelistic events but they have also sought to bring reconciliation, with justice, to their war-torn countries.[9] Few had the courage for this kind of evangelism in the Islamic world, but God still provided people like Anis Shorrosh, an Arab from Nazareth, who would be prepared to go to countries like Pakistan, Bahrain, and Kuwait.[10]

Apart from charismatic individuals, there are important agencies that have promoted highly mobile forms of mission. Operation Mobilisation has worked in some of the hardest parts of the world with teams engaged in door-to-door evangelism, as well as in equipping churches with literature and skills for their own evangelistic work. Its ships have taken young Christians all over the world, and their book exhibitions are always hugely popular because they have books on many different subjects in addition to Christian ones. It has also had the courage to address concerns about racism in some of its policies regarding the teams and has indigenized very successfully in many parts of the world.

Youth With A Mission (YWAM) is another organization which encourages teams of young people to share the gospel worldwide. They, too, have learned to work with local Christians and churches rather than going at it alone and making mistakes about culture and context which could have been avoided. In addition to the above, Christians are involved in mobile teams providing relief for those affected by natural or manmade disasters. Medical teams reach those

---

[8]See, for example, Russ Busby, *Billy Graham: God's Ambassador* (San Diego, CA: Tehabi, 1999); and Franklin Graham, *Through My Father's Eyes* (Nashville, TN: Thomas Nelson, 2018).

[9]See further, Michael Cassidy, *The Passing Summer* (London: Hodder, 1989) and his more recent *Footprints in the African Sand* (London: SPCK, 2019).

[10]James Hefley and Marti Hefley, *The Liberated Palestinian* (Wheaton, IL: Victor Books, 1980).

in remote areas with much needed treatment, and mission teams often help in the development of essential infrastructure like the building of schools, clinics, and hospitals.

Embassy and Hospitality

Both presence and peregrination are important aspects of mission and should be kept together. There are those who are called to a ministry of presence, and others who feel the urge to travel with the gospel to unfamiliar places. The history of the church shows that they are complementary and both are needed to fulfil the continuing missionary mandate which Christ has given to his church.

However, all who feel called to ministry in a fixed place should be careful to avoid the "If you build it, they will come" mentality.[11] In a church context, that means assuming if we focus on doing well what we are doing inside the church, people from outside the church will naturally want to come in and join us, without any additional effort on our part. In reality, a ministry of presence still needs to be committed to the twin tasks of *embassy* and of *hospitality*. Already in the Old Testament, the message of the servant is for the whole earth, and he is to bring light and salvation to the ends of the earth (Isa. 42:4; 49:6). The missionaries, similarly, toward the end of Isaiah, who are drawn from the nations are sent back to the nations to glorify God (Isa. 66:18-20). The New Testament is all about "sending" and "sentness." Jesus is conscious of being sent by his Father (John 8:42), and he sends his disciples into the surrounding villages and towns (Mark 6:7-13; Luke 10:1-12). After the resurrection, he sends them out into the wider world to disciple the nations (Matt. 28:18-20), and the rest of the New Testament tells us how the disciples set about doing this. Embassy, then, has to do with going out to where people are. In a parish context, for example, this may be expressed in terms of planned visitation. Such visits in people's own homes may be to prepare them for baptism, marriage, or other important events in their lives. They may be to comfort the

---

[11]For the original quotation ("If you build it, he will come") and its context, see W. P. Kinsella, *Shoeless Joe* (Boston, MA: Mariner Books, 1982), which was later made into the movie *Field of Dreams*, starring Kevin Costner.

bereaved or to attend the sick. Some places may still have some sense of a geographical parish—that is, where the local priest has an acknowledged pastoral responsibility for those who live within the parish boundaries, even if they do not attend the parish church. In such places, door-to-door visiting to offer to pray for or with people or to invite them to a celebration during a festive or solemn season can be possible. From time to time, the parish may organize a mission with events to which residents in a particular area can be invited by those who go out to visit.

Where there is an intention to plant a church, it is usually worth consulting those in the neighborhood as to what such a church might do for them. This may produce a long "wish list" from the community. Not everything that is asked for can be achieved, and there will have to be a careful balance between what the wider community wants and the needs of a fledgling congregation. Any attempt, nevertheless, at reaching out will be welcomed and allow the new church to be more at home in its surroundings and to be seen as responsive to the local situation.[12] Embassy will also involve Christians and churches in village-, town-, or city-wide events led by itinerant religious or lay evangelists or organized through local initiative. Jointly planned and run events by churches in a particular area can enhance the credibility of the Christian message among unchurched people. The Billy Graham Association, for instance, is assiduous in involving a wide range of church leaders in the planning and supporting of its missions.

The worldwide context must also be kept in mind: every congregation should have some well understood commitments to mission in other parts of the world or of the nation. This may involve sending people out, through mission agencies or independently, to pray for them, and to give toward their expenses. It may be about partnership with a congregation in a particular part of the world in assisting them in their mission—something they may be able to do more effectively than outsiders but for which they may need financial assistance, training, or other kinds of support. It may also be about bringing missionaries and evangelists from elsewhere to help us in our local mission, especially if they have skills or experience

---

[12]Michael Nazir-Ali, *Shapes of the Church to Come* (Eastbourne: Kingsway, 2001), 116–17.

which we may lack in our own situation. These may have to do with the gift for sharing the good news without inhibition or embarrassment or with knowledge of a particular ethnic or religious community or of music or dance which can commend the gospel to those around us.

Yet the embassy aspect of mission is complemented by that of hospitality. In the Old Testament, the people of the nations flow toward the house of the Lord to learn from him and to walk in his paths. This will bring about justice and peace in the world (Isa. 2:1-5; Mic. 4:1-4). We are told, moreover, that God's house is to be a "house of prayer for all the nations" (Isa. 56:6-8; cf. Mark 11:17). Jesus is portrayed in the Gospels as welcoming sinners and eating with them (Mark 2:15-18; etc.). The importance of hospitality is also underlined in the early church (Rom. 12:13; Heb. 13:2). Every church needs a well-designed strategy for welcoming people, whatever their reason for coming to church. They may come for a festival, such as Advent or Christmas, or for the baptism of a friend's child, a wedding, a funeral, or a memorial service. They may come for personal reasons like bereavement, prayer, or thanksgiving (how often have I noticed an occasional churchgoer lost in prayer in church when the regulars are chatting!). When they come, are their needs met? Are they given information about the church's activities and invited to join in? Most importantly, is there opportunity for them to hear the good news about Jesus Christ? What will they take away with them? And, very importantly, is there something for them to do that uses their skills and experience?

One of the highlights in the church's year is the summer holiday club—or Vacation Bible School, as it is sometimes known in America! So many children are sent to it by their parents, perhaps because of a nostalgia for Sunday school or because they are at work and there is nobody to look after the kids at home or even because they want to get them out of the way. Many churches, with the sacrificial help of volunteers, arrange imaginative and thought-provoking programs for children during this time. The question is about how this is followed up, both with the children themselves and with their families. At the closing event, which most such programs have, do the visiting families hear the Christian message and have some opportunity to respond? Are they given information about Sunday worship and programs for young people throughout the year? Are Sunday school teachers and youth workers at hand to answer any questions and provide information? What is the next event to which they can be invited?

Some churches are blessed with facilities which are frequently used by the wider community for a whole range of activities such as fitness clubs, music lessons, language learning, and cookery lessons. This is undoubtedly part of the ministry of hospitality, but all too often no connection is made between this use of church premises and the worshiping, witnessing life of the church. Through posters and leaflets, as well as the presence of members of the congregation and of the clergy before, during, and after such use, connections can be made and people drawn into spiritual activities—whether that is special mission services, Bible study, or prayer groups. When there are special meals together or church-sponsored outings, an epilogue toward the end, which leaves a gospel thought with those present, can be very effective. As Ann Morisy has written, we should always be seeking to add gospel value to all the things in which the local church is engaged.[13] It is true, of course, that discernment and wisdom are required for each situation as to how this is to be done, but we are not excused from doing it!

In those situations, where someone in the local church has the gift of healing through prayer and by the laying on of hands of those authorized to do it, it is vital that physical and mental healing is linked to the need for spiritual healing as well. Many come to be healed of their aches and pain or for counsel about their worries and relationships. That is great and part of the church's therapeutic task, but, with sensitivity, the whole counsel of God (Acts 20:27) needs to be brought to bear on a person's situation so that we are offering a holistic approach to healing, which includes the spiritual as well as the mental and the physical. It is worth noting, in this connection, that both *shalom* in the Old Testament and *sodzein* in the New have the sense of salvation but also of healing and wholeness.[14] The church's provision for the pastoral and sacramental care of the sick and dying should be used to its fullest effect in the course of this ministry.

---

[13]Ann Morisy, *Beyond the Good Samaritan: Community Ministry and Mission* (London: Mowbray, 1997).
[14]On embassy and hospitality, see Michael Nazir-Ali, *Citizens and Exiles: Christian Faith in a Plural World* (London: SPCK, 1998), 115–16.

It is not accidental that the success of courses like RCIA, Alpha, Christianity Explored, and Credo, which introduce people to the Christian faith, is related to the meal around which the speaking and the sharing take place. In experiencing the hospitality of Christian people and of the church, participants are led to an encounter with the hospitality of God himself. Let us then keep embassy and hospitality together in our mission thinking and practice: let us not hesitate to go walkabout for the sake of the gospel, and let us welcome people in so they may experience the gospel in the hospitality we offer.

6

Identification, Inculturation, and Dialogue

If presence is to be truly incarnational, those bringing the good news to a particular place and people will also have to be prepared to become like them as did Christ, when he took on our humanity. Showing "great humility,"[1] the only begotten of the Father came as a Palestinian Jew of the first century, and every term there has to do with the "scandal of particularity" which authentic incarnation necessarily involves. That is to say, he didn't just become generally human but assumed a humanity that was gender-, culture-, and time-specific. In his own ministry, he was ridiculed by his opponents (Matt. 13:55; Mark 6:1-6; Luke 4:22; John 7:27; 8:39-58) who could not see how this son of a carpenter could be the prophet who had been prophesied about (Deut. 18:15-22), or the promised and long-awaited Messiah and Son of God (2 Sam. 7:14; Pss. 2:7-11; 45:6, 7; 89:20-28; 110:1; etc.).

We may regard culture as uniquely an attribute of human societies which enables them to adapt to their environment and to adapt their environment to themselves, to discern social and personal meaning in existence, and to express worldviews and values which enable human beings to live together. In these ways,

---

[1] See the First Collect for Advent: "Almighty God, give us grace that we may cast away the works of darkness, and put upon us the armour of light, now in the time of this mortal life, in which thy Son Jesus Christ came to visit us in great humility . . ." Jospeh Ketley, *The Two Liturgies . . . of King Edward VI* (Cambridge: Parker Society, 1844), 41, 239; and the Ordinariates Established by *Anglicanorum Coetibus, Divine Worship* (London: CTS, 2015), 152

culture can be regarded as providential (i.e., God providing us with specific contexts and circumstances which enable us, as *Gaudium et Spes* 53 puts it, to use and develop our diverse mental, spiritual, and physical capacities). If culture is God-given in these ways and others, then it must be possible for the gospel to resonate with it, to seek to transform it, and to bring it to an awareness of its own rootedness in God's good providence.

It is such an understanding that underlies Paul's and his companions' approach to the Jewish people during their missionary journeys across the ancient world. Again and again, they show how the coming of Jesus Christ is in accordance with the Scripture and the expectation of the Jews (Acts 13:26-43; 17:1-3; 19:8-11; etc.).

When they are addressing the Gentiles, however, they appeal to whatever awareness of the divine there is in the cultural and religious background of those with whom they are dealing. Thus, to the people of Lystra, who wished to heap divine honors on Paul and Barnabas, they restrain them from such foolish idolatry and point out that they are but messengers of the one God who has not left himself without witness anywhere (Acts 14:8-17). Similarly, in his well-known encounter with the philosophers of Athens, Paul refers not only to their religious practices as a way of making a connection with the good news he is proclaiming but also to their poetical literature which witnesses to the creator God in whom we live and move and have our being (Acts 17:16-34).[2] Missiologists like Charles Kraft have drawn our attention to this approach to culture. According to him, God speaks to people in specific cultures in ways attuned to their language and cultural forms because in Christ God has identified completely with the human condition.[3] The gospel can and does bring transformation of persons, families, and cultures, but it does so from the inside, gradually and with the grain of culture rather than against it.

In commending such an approach, Kraft can be seen to be following the patristic tradition, going back to Justin Martyr (*c.* AD 150) and Clement of Alexandria (*c.* AD 200), who taught that the Logos or

---

[2]I. Howard Marshall, *The Acts of the Apostles: An Introduction and Commentary* (Leicester: IVP, 1984), 234, 281.
[3]Charles Kraft, *Christianity and Culture: A Study in Biblical Theologizing in Cross-Cultural Perspective* (New York: Orbis, 1997).

Eternal Word, incarnate in Jesus Christ, enlightens all human beings so that they can, to some extent, anticipate the coming of Christ and are thus prepared to receive the gospel when it is proclaimed to them, even if popular religion has distorted and obscured their knowledge of the truth. They need, therefore, to abjure its falsehood if they are to receive the truth in Christ.[4]

Both Scripture and these, and other, church fathers seem, then, to recognize connecting points with the surrounding culture, whether in the philosophy of the Stoics, in pagan poetry (although its falsehoods are denounced), in practical morality (such as family values), and, in the case of Clement, even in some of the prophecies of the Gentiles, which are seen as looking forward to the coming of the Christ.[5] But, of course, as we have already seen, those of the Anglican heritage are familiar with this biblical and patristic incarnational principle through "Of Ceremonies" in the preface to the *Book of Common Prayer*.[6]

The Yale scholar and African Muslim convert to Christianity and later, more specifically, to Catholicism, Lamin Sanneh also writes of the "translatability" of the gospel. It is not just that Christianity has no sacred language like Islam, for example (although it has the original and ancient languages of the Scriptures). Its Scriptures can authentically be rendered into the vernaculars of every people and nation, unlike the Qur'an. Yet its transmission goes well beyond that, in that the gospel can be expressed and make its home in the idiom and the culture of every human group. Sanneh is not afraid to point out the contrast here with Islam, which definitely has a sacred language: Arabic must be used in the recitation of the Scriptures, in ritual prayer, and in many other matters of daily life and devotion.

This circumscribes, to a significant extent, how Islamic belief, practice, and law can be rendered into the language, thought forms, and idiom of a receiving culture. Even where limited provision can be made, for example, in Shari'a Law (which is supposed to govern

---

[4]See further, Robert Sider, *The Gospel and Its Proclamation: Message of the Fathers of the Church* (Wilmington, DE: Michael Glazier, 1983), 60.
[5]Sider, *The Gospel and Its Proclamation*, 73; Michael Nazir-Ali, *The Unique and Universal Christ: Jesus in a Plural World* (Milton Keynes: Paternoster, 2008), 68.
[6]See Chapter 1.

every aspect of a believer's and a community's life), for taking account of a people's custom or *adat* (Arabic *'ada*). The Qur'an remains authoritative only in Arabic. The *Salat*, the required five-times-a-day ritual prayer, can be offered only in that language, and people can be called to such prayer only in it. As a result of the resurgence of Islam in the last century or so, the concern has not been so much about contextualization in the Islamic world as about the rapid "Arabization" of numerous cultures and peoples in the name of returning to primitive belief and practice.

Christian faith, on the other hand, for Sanneh, is inherently translatable, and it is this which makes it potentially and actually universal. This is why it spread throughout the ancient Roman and Persian empires, why "Nestorian" and other missionaries could take it as far as China and Central Asia, and why it now has a majority of adherents in Asia, Africa, and Latin America.[7]

The Japanese scholar Peter Saeki, and now Martin Palmer, have shown the extent of "Nestorian" contextualization in terms of art and architecture and of language and terminology into Chinese Taoist idiom, already by the eighth century. Their work raises many questions about how far authentic contextualization can go, but there can be no doubt of the ambitious scale on which it was undertaken by the Nestorian missionaries. We know from the wonderful account of the two Chinese monks Rabban Sauma and Markos, who were sent *from* Beijing by the then Mongol ruler Kublai Khan to worship at Jerusalem, that Nestorian Christianity was alive and well down to the thirteenth century and the beginning of the arrivals of mission from the West. It is interesting to note that Markos became patriarch of the Church of the East (the proper name for the "Nestorians") and that Rabban Sauma was sent by him to establish contact with Western Christianity.[8]

---

[7] See his magnum opus, Lamin Sanneh, *Translating the Message: The Missionary Impact on Culture*, revised edition (Maryknoll, NY: Orbis, 2009); and Sanneh, *Whose Religion Is Christianity?* (Grand Rapids, MI: Eerdmans), 2003.

[8] Peter Saeki, *The Nestorian Monument in China* (London: SPCK, 1928); and Saeki, *Nestorian Documents and Relics in China* (Tokyo: Academy of Oriental Culture, 1937). See also Martin Palmer, *The Jesus Sutras: Rediscovering the Lost Scrolls of Taoist Christianity* (New York: Ballantine, 2001); and E. A. Wallis Budge, *The Monks of Kublai Khan* (London: Religious Tract Society, 1928).

I have myself drawn attention to the way in which the ancient St. Thomas Christians of India have adapted themselves to a predominantly Hindu society, not only in terms of custom, language, and family life but even in finding themselves a place in the complex caste structure of traditional society. Again, this raises all sorts of questions about how such a group can then reach those, such as the "untouchable" Dalit, who do not enjoy the same social standing, and if they reach them, whether and how they can be integrated into the life of the church and the community. Although these are real issues, that there has been a deep engagement of the St. Thomas Christians with the surrounding culture cannot be in doubt.[9]

Sanneh himself has shown how Bible translation and mission in general have transformed, though not destroyed, African cultures and how they have made an impact on the expression of Christianity itself, both within such cultures and more widely than that. In many parts of the world, the missionary commitment to vernacularization has led to languages being transcribed for the first time, their scripts and their grammars systematized, the histories of their people being written down, and a general renewal of culture. David Gitari, the late Anglican Archbishop of Kenya, claims that the coming of Christian faith has, in many cases, preserved tribal customs and practices, and released creativity in the visual and musical arts, orienting all this activity to Christ.[10]

Since the Second Vatican Council, many in the Roman Catholic Church have come to a fresh consciousness of the importance of culture in relation to the Christian faith. In his exhortation *Evangelii Nuntiandi* (1975), Pope Paul VI was already emphasizing the importance of the gospel's relation to every human culture so that there may be a profound transformation and enrichment of

---

[9]Michael Nazir-Ali, *From Everywhere to Everywhere: A World View of Christian Mission* (London: Collins, 1991), 24; and Nazir-Ali, *Islam: A Christian Perspective* (Exeter: Paternoster, 1983), 145.

[10]Sanneh, *Translating the Message*, 191; David Gitari, "Evangelisation and Culture: Primary Evangelism in Northern Kenya," in *Proclaiming Christ in Christ's Way: Studies in Integral Evangelism*, ed. Vinay Samuel and Albrecht Hauser (Oxford: Regnum, 1989), 101–21. See also Volker Küster, "Visual Arts In World Christianity," in *The Wiley Blackwell Companion to World Christianity*, ed. L. Sanneh and M. McClymond (Oxford: Wiley, 2016), 368–85; and Frank Willett, *African Art* (London: Thames & Hudson, 1971), 44.

those cultures. John Paul II, in both *Slavorum Apostoli*, written to celebrate the eleven-hundredth anniversary of the conversion of the Slavs to Christianity, and *Redemptoris Missio*, which is about the continuing importance of mission, recognizes that there is a mutual giving and receiving in the church's encounter with cultures that enriches both sides. Benedict XVI, while still Cardinal Ratzinger, pointed out in an address to Asian bishops that the truth of the revelation in Christ leads each culture to its own true center, which is a God-given expectation of fulfillment. The culture of faith meets with particular historical cultures and, in the process, both can be enriched and transformed.[11]

In practice, this has led to liturgical experiment in appropriating cultural forms, posture, music, and so on in divine worship. It has led to an imaginative use of architecture and of taxis[12] in how worship is organized and delivered. It has affected the translation of the Bible and has brought about a new interest in doing theology in the vernacular, with terminology drawn from the spiritual and religious vocabulary of the cultures roundabout.

Those working with the poor and marginalized have sometimes drawn a distinction between culture and context. If *culture* has to do with the language, the customs, and the idiom of a particular group, *context* may be a more appropriate term for the social, economic, and political circumstances in which people live. The bringing of the good news in situations of endemic poverty, discrimination, and marginalization has to include the church's stance on these issues and how it can bring about a change in the actual condition in which people find themselves. This has been very much the thrust of "theologies of liberation" in Latin America, Asia, and Africa. It may be, as David Martin has claimed, that these theologies, in emphasizing the importance of bringing change to the

---

[11]Nazir-Ali, *The Unique and Universal Christ*, 74–6; Paul VI, *Evangelii Nuntiandi*, December 8, 1975, par. 53, *Acta Apostolicae Sedis* 68 (1976): 42; John Paul II, *Slavorum Apostoli*, June 2, 1985, par. 21, *Acta Apostolicae Sedis* 77 (1985): 802–3; John Paul II, "*Redemptoris Missio*: Encyclical Letter on the Permanent Validity of the Church's Missionary Mandate," *The Holy See*, December 7, 1990. *Catholic International* 2, no. 6 (1991): 275–7; Cardinal Ratzinger, "Christ, Faith and the Challenge of Cultures," *Origins: CNS Documentary Service* 24, no. 41 (1995): 679–86.

[12]That is, "liturgy done well."

social and economic condition of the poor, neglected people's spiritual needs. According to him, these are now being met, in some parts of the world, by the exponential growth of Pentecostalism which is also bringing about economic and social change through personal transformation and the promotion of an ethic of work, honesty, family life, and temperance.[13]

Oppressed groups, and those working among them, have expressed concern that the church's approach to inculturation has often been to engage with major religious traditions, from which the legitimation of their oppression is often drawn, rather than to focus on the spirituality of the oppressed. Thus, James Massey from north India tells us that much Indian Christian theology was written by upper-class Christians and addressed the context of classical Hinduism or Islam. Most of the people, however, come from the lowest castes and from a distinct spiritual background where they were often denied access to mainstream religious sources and places. Inculturation in their context will look very different from engaging with world religions and their accompanying cultures.[14] The spiritual experience and the religious vocabulary of the excluded masses are different from those of the religious elite and yet, where Hinduism is concerned, the church, perhaps unwittingly, has largely engaged with the literary and philosophical traditions of that faith. With Islam, similarly, the concern has largely been with the Qur'an and the written sources of the faith rather than with the popular and syncretistic faith of ordinary people.

Where mission and evangelization are concerned, the evangelists will want to relate to both the culture and the context of people groups. The evangelist will know that it is impossible to communicate the gospel without some familiarity with their language, their customs, their hopes, and their desires. At the same time, their social and economic circumstances are also relevant, if they are to see the

---

[13]On all of this, please see Michael Nazir-Ali, *Mission and Dialogue: Proclaiming the Gospel Afresh in Every Age* (London: SPCK, 1995), 29; Leonardo Boff, *Church: Charism and Power* (London: SCM, 1985); Kim Bock, ed., *Minjung Theology: People as the Subjects of History* (Singapore: Christian Conference of Asia, 1981); and David Martin, *Pentecostalism: The World Their Parish* (Oxford: Blackwell, 2002).

[14]James Massey, "Ingredients for a Dalit Theology," in *Readings in Indian Christian Theology*, ed. R. S. Sugirtharajah and Cecil Hargreaves (London: SPCK, 1993), 152–7.

gospel as being not only about acceptance of them as they are but about transformation into the wholeness which God wants for them. Both biblical words for salvation, *yeshu'ah* in Hebrew and *soteria* in Greek, imply deliverance from adverse circumstances but also a restoration to wholeness. This aspect of healing in the salvation brought by Christ should not be neglected, as we need healing at a number of levels: the physical, psychological, spiritual, and social. Our proclamation of salvation has to be directed at every aspect of the *dis*ease we find in the human condition (i.e., it needs to address both culture and context). Indeed, the proclamation must always be accompanied by programs of counselling, of befriending, of caring, and of assisting those in need of education, employment, or simply a supportive social environment.

We should not need to say that inculturation and contextualization are in the title deeds of the church and should be in its life blood. Erasmus, for example, not only produced a fresh Greek edition of the New Testament but a Latin translation of it as well. He also wrote paraphrases of nearly all the books of the New Testament and wanted everyone, including the humblest, to be able to read the Bible in their own language. Martin Luther, the German reformer, was well aware of Erasmus' work, as was William Tyndale whose sixteenth-century translation of the Bible was at the root of many other translations that followed, including the Authorized Version, which is also known as the King James Bible. This latter was also influenced by the Catholic Douai translation. Given the influence of the Bible in English on the development of the English language and its literature, it is no exaggeration to claim that it is difficult to think of a Shakespeare or a Donne or a Herbert without Tyndale, Douai, or the KJV.[15] In the same way, Thomas Cranmer's masterful rendering of the liturgy of the Church of England into English continues to stand as a standard to those enabling people to pray in their own language. The incorporation of significant parts of it into

---

[15]On the influence of Tyndale on other Bible translations, see Brian Moynihan, *William Tyndale: If God Spare My Life* (London: Abacus, 2003), 387. For his influence on the language, see David Daniell's introduction to Tyndale's *The Obedience of a Christian Man* (London: Penguin, 2000), xiii–xiv; and Rebecca Lemon, Emma Mason, Jonathan Roberts, and Christopher Rowland, eds, *The Blackwell Companion to The Bible in English Literature* (Oxford: Wiley-Blackwell, 2012).

the Ordinariates of the Catholic Church is a tribute to its quality
and beauty. The Bible in the vernacular and worship in the language
of the people are at the heart of inculturation, but the "vernacular"
is not limited to them. It should be extended to the architecture,
furnishing, and art of church buildings. It has also to do with
traditions of reverence, with music, with symbol, and with color.
How the Scriptures are read and expounded, as well as styles of
prayer and meditation, all need to be "vernacularized."

As we have noted before, "On Ceremonies" in the preface to the
Book of Common Prayer is explicit that each particular church
should be able to order its worship in ways that are most honoring
to God and edifying for the people. Article 34 of the Articles of
Religion, similarly, tells us that "traditions and ceremonies" have
always been diverse and may be changed according to the diversities
of countries, times, and manners, as long as nothing is done which
is contrary to God's word. The qualification at the end of that last
sentence is important, as it signals that there are limitations on
processes of inculturation, as well as opportunities for it. We shall
have to consider these later.

In practice, however, Anglicans have often been in thrall to
"Englishness," regardless of the cultural and geographical contexts in
which they find themselves. Rather than taking the vernacular principle
from the *Book of Common Prayer* and using it in their own linguistic
and cultural context, they have simply replicated its use, as they
have with church architecture, vestments, music, etc. In many African
contexts, I have found myself sitting through a very English prayer
book service until we have got to the offertory, and then suddenly
everything has come to life with African music (or African improvisation
of Western music), dance, and sacrificial giving! I have been left asking
why the rest of the service could not have been like that.

There have been attempts, of course, at inculturation from at least
the early years of the twentieth century. In India, for example, a liturgy
was produced which became known as the Bombay Liturgy. It was
influential in the emergence of the Liturgy for India which was
included in the *Prayer Book of the Church of India, Pakistan, Burma
and Ceylon*. Both consciously draw upon the liturgical traditions of
the ancient churches of India, one of which, the Mar Thoma Syrian
church, was in communion with them and with others they often
had good relations. Western scholars have sometimes criticized this
approach to inculturation as "contrived" and doing violence to

Anglican liturgical structure, but we have to keep in mind that the framers of these liturgies had to reckon with living traditions around them which had, for hundreds of years, taken account of their contexts, while at the same time remaining faithful to biblical and patristic faith. In fact, "Eastern" liturgical influence began to affect liturgical revision generally, in all church traditions, through the considerable impact of the *Book of Common Worship* for the Church of South India (CSI)—a church which unites Anglican, Reformed, Lutheran, and Methodist traditions. This prayer book has led the way in providing an Old Testament reading as part of the liturgy of the word, the transference of the sermon to follow the gospel and to precede the Creed, an epicletic prayer invoking the Holy Spirit over the elements, as part of the Eucharistic Prayer, but before the recitation of the Words of the Institution, old "Syrian" acclamations, and a litany form of intercessions. The Anglican Province of India, Pakistan, Burma, and Ceylon also exhibited inculturation in its liturgy, for example, by restoring the ancient *Maranatha* prayer[16] at the end of the Intercessions and by allowing local customs, such as the use of the *Mangala sutra* (an Indian marital necklace for the bride) at weddings in place of, or in addition to, the traditional ring.[17]

The CSI has more recently produced a liturgy which takes the Hindu cultural background more seriously, and the church of the Anglican Province of Kenya has now a widely known liturgy which recognizes the African sense of continuity with those who have gone before us, as well as the pastoral and agricultural life of many of its members. New Zealand has also published a prayer book which is sensitive to the needs of the Maori population and to the changing culture and context of that country and the Pacific region in general. Some of its provisions, like the use of inclusive language for God, remain controversial, but no one can deny that, in other respects, a serious attempt has been made to contextualize in a multicultural situation.[18]

---

[16]See 1 Cor. 16:22, "Our Lord, come!"

[17]See further, Colin Buchanan, ed., *Modern Anglican Liturgies 1958–1968* (Oxford: Oxford University Press, 1968); and Buchanan, *Further Anglican Liturgies 1968–1975* (Nottingham: Grove Books, 1975).

[18]Wendy Robins, ed., *Let All the World: Liturgies, Litanies and Prayers from Around the World* (London: USPG, 1990); and *A New Zealand Prayer Book* (Auckland: Collins, 1989).

In the Catholic Church, the Second Vatican Council, in its Constitution on the Sacred Liturgy *Sacrosanctum Concilium*, set in train a radical process of vernacularization and inculturation which has led not only to the simplification of rites but greater participation of the laity in the Mass, as also in the celebration of the other sacraments and in other kinds of corporate worship. This process has most affected the Latin rite but I have noticed its influence also on the oriental rites and, indeed, on the liturgies of other churches. The newer liturgies complement and do not oppose the traditional ones.

Attitudes to worship, gestures, and posture play a very important part in the inculturation of worship. The dramatic gesture of "sending all our sins to the cross of Christ" in the Anglican Kenyan liturgy is an example which is becoming familiar to many throughout the Anglican Communion. In South Asia, the ministers and the congregation often remove their shoes at the celebration of the Eucharist as a sign of reverence. In India, the Peace can be given in the form of the *Namaste* greeting. This enables people to greet each other across the sex divide without having to touch someone of the opposite sex—something still not usual in traditional settings. In Korea, on the other hand, the president and the people bow to one another at the Peace.

All attempts at understanding and accommodating to cultures and contexts depends on a profound and continuing dialogue with the people and their traditions, customs, values, and worldview as a whole. Such dialogue is not limited to "official" circles, such as religious leaders or academics, but must take place at every level: among neighbors, colleagues at work, and students. One reason for dialogue is simply to discover "what makes people tick," their background, beliefs, hopes, and fears. When people of different faiths meet, it is natural for them to want to discover what each believes and where there may be similarities and differences between them. This is sometimes known as "discursive" dialogue. It requires patient listening to the other, but it also requires some ability to give an account of our own faith. This can be done without compromise and without inhibition. The other wants to hear about what we believe, just as we wish to know what they hold dear in their faith.

In this connection, it is worth noting that the great missionary pioneers of the eighteenth and nineteenth centuries gave considerable time not only to the learning of languages but also in getting to know the spiritual beliefs and traditions of the people they were trying to reach. One of the earliest group of missionaries to reach India from England were

the Baptists: William Carey the Shoemaker (1761–1834) and only a
  little later Joshua Marshman the Schoolmaster (1768–1837) and
William Ward the Printer (1769–1823). Because of the hostile policies of
the East India Company, they had to face many vicissitudes and
experience failure, as well as success. Although they believed strongly
in the uniqueness of the Christian faith, they knew also that they had
to enter the Hindu thought world of those they were trying to reach.
Carey didn't just translate the Bible into Sanskrit, Bengali, and Marathi.
He also produced a Sanskrit grammar and translated the *Ramayana*
into English! Ward, similarly, published his work on the manners and
customs of his Hindu interlocutors. The opening of Serampore College
(now University) was explicitly for the promotion of Eastern literature
and European science—an approach quite different from the now
notorious remark by T. B. Macaulay (1800–58), the British politician
and historian, that one shelf of European works was of more worth than
all the literature of the East![19]

The approach taken by the Baptists in early nineteenth-century
India was also taken by Anglicans in the early twentieth in the
Middle East. The names most associated with this new approach
are Temple Gairdner and his distinguished colleague, Constance
Padwick. They wanted to turn away from an atmosphere of polemic,
debate, and disputation to one where a genuine attempt was made
to understand the wellsprings of the spiritual aspirations of
Muslims. A stream of literature flowed from the CMS in Egypt
which sought to present Christ as the fulfillment of the hopes and
aspirations of Muslims. To be able to do this effectively, it was
necessary to understand what these were. This required research,
translation, and writing of the highest order.[20]

The famous British-German orientalist, Max Müller (1823–
1900), did perhaps more than anyone to make the sacred books of
the East available to a Western readership. He said in a speech to

---

[19]Stephen Neill, *A History of Christian Missions* (Harmondsworth: Penguin, 1986),
223.
[20]Examples of this are W. H. T. Gairdner's translation of Al Ghazzali's *Mishkat Al
Anwar as the Niche for Lights* (London: Royal Asiatic Society, 1924); and Constance
Padwick's *Muslim Devotions: A Study of Prayer-Manuals in Common Use* (London:
SPCK, 1961). See further, Gordon Hewitt, *The Problems of Success: A History of the
Church Missionary Society 1910–1942, Vol. 1: In Tropical Africa, The Middle East,
At Home* (London: SCM Press, 1971), 315.

the Bible Society that we must not reject whatever is true and noble in these books but that, in the final analysis, they all taught salvation by works. It was only one book from the East, the Bible, which teaches that salvation is through faith and that good works flow out from such faith. Here is an example of profound engagement but also of clear witness to the unique authority of the Bible.[21]

Some who began to engage in dialogue with the people and the literature of other religions came to espouse a theology of "fulfillment." They believed that just as Christ had fulfilled the hopes and expectations in the Old Testament, so also he could fulfill at least certain aspects of the spiritual aspirations and implications found in the sacred writings of other religions. Toward the end of the nineteenth century, the aim of writers like J. N. Farquhar and T. E. Slater was to show that Christianity was not about replacing the different religious traditions but to fulfill their noblest longings. A more recent example of this tendency is the work of Father Raimundo Pannikar. In his now well-known work *The Unknown Christ of Hinduism*, he inquires as to how the "Christic" question is asked and answered in classical Hinduism. That is to say, how a relationship is established between Absolute Transcendence and the phenomenal, mundane world of the day to day. For Panniker, such thought is a *praeparatio evangelica*[22] for talking to Hindus about God's relationship to the eternal Logos and the incarnation of the Logos in the man Jesus Christ.[23] At their best, such theologies wish to see Christian faith as deeply related to the fundamental longings of people of other faiths, but there is always the danger of regarding people of other faiths as somehow "anonymous Christians after all" and of not having enough respect for the integrity of other worldviews.

In an evangelical theology of religions, Daniel Strange challenges "uncritical" fulfillment-type theologies. For him, the gospel confronts,

---

[21]Daniel Strange, *For Their Rock Is Not Like Our Rock: An Evangelical Theology of Religions* (Nottingham: Apollos, 2014), 8.

[22]That is, "a preparation for the gospel."

[23]J. N. Farquhar, *The Crown of Hinduism* (Oxford: Oxford University Press, 1913); Eric Sharpe, *Not to Destroy but to Fulfil* (Uppsala: Gleerup, 1965); and Raimundo Pannikar, *The Unknown Christ of Hinduism* (London, Darton Longman & Todd, 1964).

challenges, and rejects all that is false and "idolatrous" in religious traditions. This is the "subversive" effect of the proclamation of the good news. There is, however, also a fulfillment aspect to the gospel. Because of the *imago Dei*,[24] common grace, and awareness of the moral law—however distorted and obscured they may be in a fallen humanity—there is an "attachment point" in all people to the very source of their being. The questions that are asked in other religions about authentic being, true knowledge, and right moral behavior, but which cannot be satisfactorily answered within their framework, are answered by the definitive revelation of the triune God who is Creator, Savior, and Sanctifier. Strange calls this "subversive fulfilment," from a phrase first used by the great missiologist Hendrik Kraemer (1888–1965).[25] Although there may be no continuity between the gospel and man-made religion, there is continuity between what gives rise to religious belief—namely, God's revelation of himself in creation and in conscience—and our spiritual quest. However critical we may be of actual religious traditions, if we are to be effective communicators of the gospel, we must be able to recognize and use this connection between human beings and their maker.

Not only in the so-called world religions but also in primal expressions of religion there can be anticipations of biblical revelation and the gospel. Although these can be obscured or distorted, they can also offer more fruitful "connecting points" than secular worldviews. In very different contexts and in different ways, both John V. Taylor, a distinguished predecessor of mine as General Secretary of the CMS and then Bishop of Winchester, and Don Richardson, the intrepid missionary, offer us insights into the worldviews of cultures where the spiritual is important, even preeminent, and their relationship to the gospel.[26] It is most important to understand those elements in a culture which may hinder the cause of the gospel and those which may illumine and confirm it. Myths, dedicated individuals (like the peace child during

---

[24]That is, "the image of God" found in humanity according to Gen. 1:26.

[25]Strange, *For Their Rock Is Not Like Our Rock*, 266.

[26]John V. Taylor, *The Go-Between God* (London: Student Christian Ministry, 1995); Taylor, *The Christlike God* (London: Student Christian Movement, 2004); Taylor, *The Primal Vision* (London: Student Christian Movement, 2004); and Don Richardson, *Peace Child* (Ada, MI: Bethany House, 2005).

whose life peace is maintained between warring tribes), symbols, and sacred rites may all point to their fulfillment in Christ.

One question that often arises, in the context of mission and dialogue, is what term Christians should use for God. The problem is already found in the Bible: the Hebrew term *El* can be used for the gods of the nations and even, it seems, for god-like humans and yet can also be used, with the Hebrew article *Ha*, for the only and true God, even alongside the divine tetragrammaton[27] (e.g., Ps. 18:31; Isa. 42:5). Melchizedek is described as priest of *El 'Elyon*, or "God Most High." He blesses the name of God Most High and blesses Abram (as he then was) in the name of God Most High. Abram then offers him a tithe of all he has (Gen. 14:18-20). In the Septuagint, the Greek translation of the Older Testament, which was the Bible of the early church, *Ho Theos* is used for *Ha-El* in the full knowledge that the term could be and was used for pagan gods and, indeed, in variant forms, for goddesses (Gen. 1:1 and passim). This usage of referring to the God of the Bible as *Theos*, with or without the article, continues in the New Testament (Matt. 1:23; John 1:18 and passim). The same can be said of the Aramaic/Syriac *Alaha* and of the Latin *Deus*. They can refer both to the true God and to the diverse deities of Levantine or Greco-Roman paganism.

William Carey is celebrated for initiating a deep study of classical Indian literature, including religious literature. His purpose in doing so was, of course, to discover appropriate terminology in which to communicate the gospel to Hindus. He revised his translation of the Bible into Bengali several times. In doing so, he had to choose which word for God to use. Because his orientation was toward Hinduism and Sanskrit, he chose *Ishwar*, a term used to refer to the Supreme Being thought of in personal terms. This use certainly reached Hindu Bengalis, but it gave Muslim Bengalis the impression that Christianity was some kind of Hindu sect! This impression was not corrected until a version of the New Testament was produced late in the twentieth century using Muslim terminology.[28]

I remember being in Zimbabwe as the preacher on the occasion of the centenary of Bernard Mizeki's martyrdom. This Mozambican

---

[27]That is, the four consonants that are used together in the Hebrew Bible to indicate the unpronounced personal name of God, i.e., YHWH.

[28]Neill, *A History of Christian Missions*, 223; Nazir-Ali, *From Everywhere to Everywhere*, 74, 158–9.

apostle to the Shona people was most interested in discovering the spiritual vocabulary of the people and, in particular, their belief in the Great Spirit, *Mwari*. It was illuminating, therefore, to see how this has become the ordinary word for God among Christians and is thus regularly used in the liturgy. The East African scholar John Mbiti has shown how belief in a supreme being is ubiquitous in pre-modern Africa, and the great Ghanaian missiologist Kwame Bediako tells us that in virtually every Christian community in Africa, the Christian term for God is usually the pre-Christian name for the Supreme Being.[29]

This brings us to the hotly contested topic of the use of *Allah* by Christians and the relation of the God of the Qur'an to the God of the Bible. It is clear that the term *Allah* was already in use among the Arabs in pre-Islamic Arabia. It has been suggested that it is a loanword adapted from the Christian Aramaic *Alaha*, or that it emerged when the different tribes came together for pilgrimages and the god of each, *al-ilah*, came to be seen as the common deity of all. There is another possibility, however: John Mbiti has shown that in primal traditions, the name for the Supreme Being is often older than the names for lesser divinities, spirits, ancestors, etc. and can be shared among what are now diverse cultures and languages. If this is applied to pre-Islamic Arabia, it raises the possibility that the term *Allah* is not an import, nor is it a development out of the tribes coming together, but that it may, as in Africa, belong to a primal monotheism that was later corrupted into polytheism.[30]

Whatever we may say of the prehistory, it cannot be denied that *Allah* comes to the fore in the Qur'an as the deity who reveals himself to Muhammad, the Prophet of Islam. The Qur'anic doctrine of God is quite different from the biblical and the Christian. Here is a God who is utterly transcendent and who cannot be known. Only what he reveals of his will, his commands and prohibitions, can be known and must be obeyed. In spite of some ambiguities, his unity is thought of as numerical rather than relational, and the

---

[29]J. S. Mbiti, *Introduction to African Religion* (Nairobi: Heinemann, 1991), 45; Kwame Bediako, *Christianity in Africa: The Renewal of a Non-Western Religion* (New York: Orbis, 1995), 97; Michael Nazir-Ali, *Citizens and Exiles: Christian Faith in a Plural World* (London: SPCK, 1998), 15.

[30]See further, Nazir-Ali, *Citizens and Exiles*, 17–18.

Christian doctrine of the Trinity, as well as the divinity of Christ, are explicitly denied. Those who assert that the doctrine of *Allah* in the Qur'an and the biblical view of God are incompatible have a strong case.[31]

In the light of these significant differences, should Christians use the term *Allah* for God? We know that Christians writing in Arabic were using this term from the earliest period, and translations of the Bible into Arabic—again from the earliest to our own times—use the term for God. This is also true of liturgy, preaching, apologetics, prayer, and devotion.[32] What needs saying is that Arabic-speaking Christians do not use the word in its Islamic sense. As with all other languages, and their terms for the Supreme Being, they infuse it with a biblical and Christian sense that is quite distinct from its Qur'anic meaning.

My own experience of those who come to faith in Christ from a Muslim background is that they often see their experience of God while still Muslims—however ill-defined and even distorted—as preparing them for the good news of the gospel. They can see their conversion as completion, correction, and even transformation, but there is not total rejection of what has gone before. As the well-known late Anglican Bishop in Iran, Hasan Dehqani-Tafti (himself a convert) states,

> Some people tend to think that Muslims have one God and Christians another. While I agree that the two concepts are very different indeed from each other, I cannot agree that they really worship two utterly different gods ... I never had a complete "brainwash," as it were, of my past faith in God; neither did I think it was necessary to do so. It was when I really put my trust in God that I started to study and experience the different conceptions of Him in the two religions.[33]

---

[31] For example, see Sam Solomon, *Not the Same God: Is the Qur'anic Allah the Lord God of the Bible?* (London: Wilberforce Publications, 2016).

[32] Sidney H. Griffith, *The Bible in Arabic* (Princeton, NJ: Princeton University Press, 2013); Griffith, *The Church in the Shadow of their Mosque* (Princeton, NJ: Princeton University Press, 2008); Mark Beaumont, *Christology in Dialogue with Muslims* (Oxford: Regnum, 2005).

[33] H. B. Dehqani-Tafti, *Design of My World* (London: Lutterworth, 1959), 66–7.

Bishop Kenneth Cragg, who was for long the doyen of Christian scholarship on Islam, similarly recognizes that there are very significant differences between Christian and Muslim accounts of God, but he claims that there are similarities and continuities as well. Christians and Muslims may together affirm some of God's attributes, such as his omnipotence, omniscience, and mercy, while disagreeing about others, such as suffering, humility, and incarnation. Cragg believes that, in grammatical terms, this is disagreement about the predicates of the same subject.[34] On the other hand, Arne Rudvin, the late Church of Pakistan Bishop of Karachi, held that the way in which Christians understand the nature and attributes of God is so radically different from Islam that we cannot easily think that we are speaking of the same being.[35] Even with supposedly shared beliefs about the unity of God, prophecy, or revelation, the ways in which these are understood are so different in Islam and Christianity that the similarity is more verbal than real.

When Muslims talk about God, however, it is not always with Islamic doctrine in mind but in terms of what Christians would call general revelation in creation and conscience. It is interesting to note that many languages spoken by Muslims retain words for God other than *Allah*. In this sense, certainly, however incomplete or distorted such an understanding may be, from a Christian point of view, it is possible to converse, and even to witness, on the basis that we are talking about the Supreme Being, the maker of heaven and earth and of ourselves, the one who has implanted a knowledge of his will in human hearts, however much fallen humans have obscured and distorted it (Acts 14:15-17; 17:22-31; Rom. 1:18-23; 2:12-16).

In some Patristic, Reformed, and Catholic thought, there is also the notion of *Prisca Theologia*—that is to say, a certain amount of God's special revelation to the ancients has been preserved in all

---

[34]Kenneth Cragg, "Islamic Theology: Limits and Bridges," in *The Gospel and Islam*, ed. D. M. McCurry (Monrovia, CA: Missions Advanced Research and Communication Center, 1979), 198.

[35]Arne Rudvin, "The Gospel and Islam: What Sort of Dialogue is Possible?," *Al-Mushir: Theological Journal of the Christian Study Centre, Rawalpindi, Pakistan* 21, nos. 3–4 (Autumn 1979): 94.

cultures and even religious traditions. This can work as *praeparatio evangelica*,[36] which enables a response to Christian evangelism when it takes place.[37] While always being alert to the corruption of whatever knowledge of God people may have, the above discussion gives us some ground for recognizing a certain amount of commonality and continuity in dialogue with partners of other faiths and of none, and in bearing faithful witness to them.

In addition, then, to discursive dialogue, there is also what has been called the "dialogue of the heart," where people share their spiritual experiences with one another. It is well known that the Prophet of Islam was very taken with the Christian monks and hermits of the Egyptian, Syrian, and Mesopotamian deserts. Thus, the Qur'an declares that Christians are the nearest to Muslims in love, and this is because they have among them monks and priests and they are not arrogant (5:85). Even Muslim scholars allow that the pioneers of Sufism or Islamic mysticism were influenced by the example of Christian monasticism, even if, later on, Neo-Platonic, Hindu, and Buddhist influence cannot be discounted.[38]

There has also been significant, and more recent, dialogue of this kind between Christians and Hindus, and Christians and Buddhists. With Hindus, names like the Benedictine Bede Griffiths, with his Christian *ashram* movement, and Swami Abhishiktananda, also a Benedictine, come to mind. The latter has written of the encounter of the heart where Hindus and Christians can ponder together the deepest mysteries. For Christians, these are revealed in the face of Jesus Christ, whereas for Hindus they have as yet no face.

The encounter of the American Cistercian monk Thomas Merton (1915–68) with the Buddhist mystical tradition is well known. His concern was whether traditions other than Christian can question or even illuminate the Christian spiritual quest. There are obvious dangers of syncretism and compromise in these approaches,

---

[36]That is, "a preparation for the gospel."
[37]See further, Strange, *For Their Rock Is Not Like Our Rock*, 95; and Adam Sparks, *One of a Kind: The Relationship between Old and New Covenants* (Eugene, OR: Pickwick, 2010), 270.
[38]Muhammad Iqbal, *The Development of Metaphysics in Persia* (Lahore: Bazm-i-Iqbal, 1964), 76.

but there cannot be true contextualization if the deepest spiritual longings and resources of people are not taken into account.[39]

An Anglican example of such encounter with the Hindu and Buddhist traditions can be found in the letters between Max Warren, General Secretary of CMS in the middle years of the twentieth century, and his son-in-law, Roger Hooker, who along with his wife, Warren's daughter, Pat, was a CMS Mission Partner in the Hindu holy city of Varanasi or Benares. Although the letters range far and wide on questions of interfaith encounter in general, they also manifest a deep awareness of the need for a spiritual encounter between believers from different traditions and how an encounter with Christ might transform the spirituality of India from the inside.[40] All of this goes well beyond inculturation of external forms and even of language. It seeks to express the Christian faith in terms of the spiritual awareness and even insights of another tradition and culture, and, most importantly, in response to its deepest longings. In terms of the Anglican tradition, we find that the stated aim of the early Anglicans was to reconnect the promises of the gospel with the desires found in "the deepness" of the human heart and transform them thereby.[41] This is also what missiologists like John Taylor, Max Warren, and Roger Hooker are trying to express in their dealings with the diverse spiritual heritage of the human race.

Another reason for dialogue is the need to build up peaceful communities with a commitment to harmonious coexistence and

---

[39]For a convenient summary of the many aspects of spiritual dialogue, see Kenneth Cracknell, *Towards a New Relationship: Christians and People of Other Faith* (London: Epworth, 1986), 128. On Buddhist–Christian relations, see Elizabeth Harris, *What Buddhists Believe* (Oxford: One World, 1998); and Nazir-Ali, *From Everywhere to Everywhere*, 153.

[40]Graham Kings, *Christianity Connected: Hindus, Muslims and the World in the Letters of Max Warren and Roger Hooker* (Zoetermeer: Boekcentrum, 2002).

[41]"But, if the profession of our faith of the remission of our own sins enter within us into the deepness of our hearts, then it must needs kindle a warm fire of love in our hearts towards God, and towards all other for the love of God,—a fervent mind to seek and procure God's honour, will, and pleasure in all things,—a good will and mind to help every man and to do good unto them, so far as our might, wisdom, learning, counsel, health, strength, and all other gifts which we have received of God, will extend,—and, in summa, a firm intent and purpose to do all that is good, and leave all that is evil," Thomas Cranmer to Henry VIII, in J. E. Cox, *The Miscellaneous Writings and Letters of Thomas Cranmer* (Cambridge: Parker Society, 1846), 86.

cooperation in the development of such communities. I well remember a Muslim Sheikh and his Christian friend telling us in Kenya how the two communities help each other in their "*Harambee*," or self-help projects. Such cooperation can lead to dialogue about the wellsprings of belief in each community which lead to cooperation, as well as to an acknowledgement of distinctives.[42] In Pakistan, similarly, the Franciscans established a center in an ordinary flat on a large housing estate in the city of Karachi. The center was open to all. Free coaching was offered to school children, and there was a place for prayer and meditation. Questions about human rights, justice, and freedom began to be raised and these, in turn, led to a dialogue about the spiritual basis for our commitment to these personal and social goods.[43] The Anglican Diocese in Egypt runs some schools and health care programs along with Muslim partners. According to them, this has increased social harmony and created a basis for dialogue about matters of faith. Many other examples can be given regarding cooperation and dialogue for the sake of cohesion and development.

More recently, with the resurgence of religious extremism of different kinds, there has been a desire for people of different faiths to discuss the nature of fundamental human freedoms, what their faiths teach about them, and their own commitment in this matter. On some occasions, this discussion has taken place around the UN Universal Declaration of Human Rights and especially Article 18, which guarantees "freedom of thought, conscience and religion," including the right to change one's religion and to manifest this religion in public or in private.[44] Where Roman Catholics have been involved, the Second Vatican Council's Declaration on religious liberty, *Dignitatis Humanae*, has also featured as a basis for such dialogue. As Colin Chapman has noted, a number of attempts have been made at articulating declarations of human rights for the Islamic world, but they have been notable for the absence of an equivalent to Article 18 of the UN Declaration. I have myself been involved in dialogues regarding fundamental freedoms, with varying

---

[42]Nazir-Ali, *Islam: A Christian Perspective*, 150. See also David Shenk and Badru Kateregga, *Islam and Christianity: A Muslim and a Christian in Dialogue* (Grand Rapids, MI: Eerdmans, 1981).

[43]Nazir-Ali, *From Everywhere to Everywhere*, 143.

[44]United Nations General Assembly, *Universal Declaration of Human Rights*, Paris, December 10, 1948.

results. In the dialogue with Al-Azhar Al-Sharif in Cairo, the premier place of Sunni learning in the world, the need for freedom of belief in the UN Article 18 sense came increasingly to be recognized. This has been a welcome development and needs now to be acknowledged in terms of law and practice in Egypt and beyond. With Shi'a scholars in Iran, there has been much less success. While they are willing to accept that there should be freedom of religion for the country's religio-ethnic minorities, there is significant resistance to any recognition of the right of people to change their religion except where they convert to Islam! Government-sponsored dialogues, like the US Secretary of State's and the British government's "Ministerials", are also engaging with questions of religious freedom. This kind of dialogue will become more and more important as minorities from many religious groups are threatened by religious or nationalist extremism.[45]

We see, then, that dialogue is necessary for effective missionary engagement with cultures and the worldview that underlies them. Not only does this help Christians to develop a proper awareness of the language, thought forms, attitudes of reverence, and many other features of the cultures in the midst of which they are placed, but it should be our hope that it also helps people in that culture to find its true center and to lead to that fulfillment which they desire. At a more personal level, dialogue can be about the sharing of our deepest experiences and spiritual aspirations, and it can also be about building community and about protecting fundamental freedoms, including freedom of belief. Above all, from the Christian point of view, dialogue is for the sake of communicating the good news of Jesus Christ and for the planting of Christian communities familiar with the spiritual and cultural idiom of the people they are seeking to reach and among whom they are placed.

---

[45]See the UN General Assembly's *Universal Declaration of Human Rights* (New York: UN Office of Public Information, 1973), 5–6; Austin Flannery OP, ed., *Vatican Council II: The Conciliar and Post Conciliar Documents* (Northport, NY: Costello, 1987), 799; Colin Chapman, *Islam and the West: Conflict, Coexistence or Conversion?* (Carlisle: Paternoster, 1998), 123; and Michael Ipgrave, *The Road Ahead: A Christian–Muslim Dialogue* (London: Church House Publishing, 2002).

7

Are There Limits
to Inculturation?

There have always been questions about how far inculturation can go. As we have seen, Article 34 of the Anglican Articles of Religion specifically limited gospel accommodation to local culture with the significant caveat, "so that nothing be ordained against God's word." What, then, is authentically a conveying of the good news in terms which people can understand and accept, and what is compromise or even capitulation? When the Council of Jerusalem decreed in circa AD 50 that Gentile converts to the Christian faith were not required to become Jews as a condition of becoming Christian, it laid down some minimal criteria about refraining from idolatry and immorality for these converts. It also required them not to eat certain things so that table fellowship between Jews and Gentiles could be possible. It goes without saying, however, that many other matters about worship of the one God of the Jewish Scriptures, the rejection of the imperial cult, the primacy of confessing Jesus as Lord, and a readiness to receive the Holy Spirit would all have been assumed.[1]

We have seen already the tension between those missionaries in Europe who wished to accommodate to some aspects of pagan culture and those who were adamantly opposed. Thus, Gregory the Great's famous letter directed to St. Augustine of Canterbury instructed him to retain the pagan shrines and, after purification,

---

[1]I. Howard Marshall, *The Acts of the Apostles: An Introduction and Commentary* (Leicester: IVP, 1984), 242.

put them to Christian use. St. Boniface, the English missionary to the Germans, on the other hand, was assiduous in destroying sacred trees and pagan shrines.[2] Even Gregory's letter provided for inculturation with certain restrictions to guard against syncretism.

Are there limits, then, to inculturation or criteria by which authentic inculturation can be distinguished from mere accommodation? In his landmark encyclical on the continuing missionary mandate of the church, *Redemptoris Missio*, Pope John Paul II encourages the process of inculturation. In this process, the church makes the gospel meaningfully present in different cultures but also welcomes peoples, with their cultures and customs, into her own community. She transmits gospel values to them while, at the same time, taking good elements from these cultures and renewing them from within so that the gospel can be better understood and lived in those cultures.

There are, however, limits to this process: whatever is done must be compatible with the nature of the gospel itself and, secondly, it should not hinder fellowship among churches and Christians in widely different situations. If the gospel is taken to be the whole of God's plan for his creation, this must mean that inculturation does not detract in any way from the narratives of creation, fall, redemption, election in Christ, sanctification, and glorification. At the same time, our inculturation into our culture should be recognizable as authentically evangelical by other churches and Christians, just as theirs should be thus recognizable to us. Truly inculturated expressions of the gospel in various cultures will eventually be seen to be in harmony with one another, even if there are tensions and questions along the way.[3]

This is one of the reasons, of course, for what the creeds call the "Catholic" church: a worldwide and across-the-ages fellowship of Christians and churches where there is mutual discernment of the truth about aspects of Christian belief or of living the Christian life, the possibility of mutual correction and complementarity, and some

---

[2]Bede, *The Ecclesiastical History of the English People* (Oxford: Oxford University Press, 2008), 56–7; Anton Wessels, *Europe: Was it Ever Really Christian?* (London: Student Christian Movement, 1994), 102–3.

[3]John Paul II, "*Redemptoris Missio*: Encyclical Letter on the Permanent Validity of the Church's Missionary Mandate," *The Holy See*, December 7, 1990. *Catholic International* 2, no. 6 (1991): 275–7.

agreement about how the gospel can be proclaimed both distinctively and unitedly in diverse cultures. In our day, the challenge for the Anglican Communion, in this respect, is to renounce the idea of the radical autonomy of local churches, which has been foisted upon it by Western churches in thrall to their culture, and to return to the truly catholic idea as set out at the 1920 Lambeth Conference, which speaks of the independence of Christian freedom, which, nevertheless, recognizes the restraints of truth and love.[4] "In essentials unity, in non-essentials liberty, in all things charity" must be the ancient principle which guides us in the choppy waters of relativism and revisionism. The churches together must decide, through their authentic teachers, what the church has "always, everywhere, and by all" (*semper, ubique, et ab omnibus*) believed the Bible teaches and "what questions touch the life of all so that they must be decided upon by all" (*quod omnes tangit ab omnibus approbatur*). Both GAFCON and the Global South movements for orthodoxy in the Anglican Communion are struggling to have these fundamental principles recognized, if there is to be a genuine fellowship in the gospel for the future, but, in the absence of an effective magisterium and a commonly acknowledged body of teaching, can their heroic efforts succeed?

The World Council of Churches has also had a program on the gospel and culture directed by the Indian theologian Christopher Duraisingh. This culminated in a conference on mission and evangelism in Salvador, Brazil. Rather than emphasizing limits on inculturation and contextualization, the program sought rather to identify criteria for the authentic transmission and living out of the radical demands of the gospel in various cultures. We should ask, therefore, whether the mind of Christ or of the Scriptures is being conveyed in the context of a particular culture, both in terms of affirming what is true and life-enhancing and of challenging anything that denies the humanity and its flourishing, especially of oppressed and marginalized groups. Is the gospel being made more intelligible by the process? Is it able to touch the heart and to inspire the people of a particular culture? Does it inform the process of change which is required for social and spiritual transformation?

---

[4]Encyclical Letter, Lambeth Conference, 1920, in G. R. Evans and J. R. Wright, eds, *The Anglican Tradition: A Handbook of Sources* (London: SPCK, 1991), 383.

On the one hand, the process seeks to convey the whole of Christ's mind as it has been revealed to the church. On the other, it recognizes that there are important trajectories in the Bible of providence, liberation, and spirituality that may appeal to those of specific cultures.[5]

Although the emphases are different in the two approaches, one emphasizes congruence with the nature of the gospel itself and the need for unity among God's people, while the other lays stress on the liberating power of the gospel; both exclude certain forms of inculturation as compromising the gospel.

Gospel and Culture

Richard Niebuhr, in his seminal and still-important work, *Christ and Culture*, attempted to show the different ways in which the gospel can relate to particular cultures. Thus, there is the Christ *of* or *for* culture, where the gospel informs the beliefs, values, customs, and laws of a culture. It also provides a means of critique if the culture strays too far from such beliefs and values. Western Christendom, Byzantium, Armenia, and Ethiopia may be taken as examples of where there was an explicit acknowledgement of what the culture owed to the Christian tradition, however much it may have strayed from its foundational principles. Christ is also *above* every culture in the sense that no culture can fully express all the riches of the gospel. Personal faith, the sacraments of the church, and a rich interior life are needed if we are to access all that Christ has to offer. It is true that the gospel does not leave any culture that it encounters as it is but brings about a profound transformation which allows what is best and most creative in a culture to be expressed. According to Niebuhr, however, there have been, and always will be, occasions when the gospel will be *against* culture, when, for instance, it denies the reality of providence or purpose or the equal value of every human person. In the name of the good news, then, Christians will have to oppose all that is God- and life-denying.[6]

---

[5]Christopher Duraisingh, ed., *Called to One Hope: The Gospel in Diverse Cultures* (Geneva: World Council of Churches, 1998).
[6]H. Richard Niebuhr, *Christ and Culture* (London: Faber & Faber, 1952).

As we have seen, the late Archbishop David Gitari of Kenya was a stalwart upholder of the need for inculturation, but in the very address that we looked at earlier, he recognizes those inescapable situations where Christians and churches, in the name of the gospel, must challenge cultural assumptions and practices that are contrary to God's providence in creation, to the moral law embedded in our consciences and elaborated in the Bible, and to the plain teaching of Christ.[7]

In a faith which is both global and increasingly at home in many different cultures, the proposers and practitioners of inculturation will have to be very attentive to the dangers of presenting the good news of salvation only partially because of scruples about the culture or because Christianity is seen as too difficult or because a culture is instinctively syncretistic, seeking to assimilate rather than to oppose. They may also have to resist the temptation of "easy pickings" by not laying out clearly the demands of the gospel, as well as the grace that accompanies them, for those who profess faith in Christ and his work for us.

The Jesuit Roberto de Nobili (1577–1656) experimented boldly in creating an "Indian rite" which took full account of Indian customs and was orientated to reaching the upper castes. While there was toleration, and even approval, from Rome regarding the adoption of Indian dress, food, and even language, Nobili's desire to allow upper caste Indians to be segregated from lower caste Christians was much more controversial. Although some of his converts survived, he was withdrawn from the mission, and, in fact, it was only when the lower castes began coming to faith that something like a mass movement began. While Nobili's sacrificial work cannot be minimized, in the end the *sensus fidelium*[8] has been that neither caste nor race can be the basis for a local church, even if people from a similar family, professional, or cultural background can gather for fellowship, study, and prayer in ways similar to the churches in people's homes that are mentioned in the New Testament

---

[7]David Gitari, "Evangelisation and Culture: Primary Evangelism in Northern Kenya," in *Proclaiming Christ in Christ's Way: Studies in Integral Evangelism*, ed. Vinay Samuel and Albrecht Hauser (Oxford: Regnum, 1989), 105–21.

[8]That is, "the sense of the faithful," where there is universal agreement by the whole body of Christ on matters of faith and morals.

but which are distinct from the larger gatherings in towns and cities to which many of the letters of the New Testament are addressed (given that these, too, may originally have met in the homes of believers).[9]

What Nobili was doing in India was also being done in China. His fellow Jesuit and near-contemporary Matteo Ricci (1552–1610) adopted Chinese vocabulary to convey the Christian message. He used Chinese for worship and held that honors paid to Confucius and the ancestors were merely "civil honors" and should not be confused with pagan worship. At first, this proved acceptable to the Chinese and was approved by Rome. In the end, however, Rome judged Ricci and his successors also to have compromised and the concessions were rescinded. One of the reasons for the eventual suppression of the order in the eighteenth century had to do with their approach to contextualization. From our point of view, we can see that much of what the Jesuits were doing was authentic inculturation, opposed by the then Roman Curia's monocultural approach. On the other hand, there were certainly features of their work which could legitimately be criticized for syncretism and compromise.[10]

The Church in the Home, the Parish, and the World

More recently, there have been missiologies which have argued that people become Christians more easily within their social, ethnic, or even professional grouping. In one sense, this is not controversial. We have missions to students, sports people, housing estates, and language groups. We have seen also how such groups, when they have been reached, can express their faith and their worship alongside others from a similar background on analogy with the New Testament churches of the household which show a "family likeness," although the household would not have been anything

---

[9]See Stephen Neill, *A History of Christian Missions* (Harmondsworth: Penguin, 1986), 156; and Michael Nazir-Ali, *The Unique and Universal Christ: Jesus in a Plural World* (Milton Keynes: Paternoster, 2008), 79.
[10]Neill, *A History of Christian Missions*, 160.

like the contemporary nuclear family but would have included extended relatives, servants, and slaves (Rom. 16:5; Col. 4:15; Philem. 2). Such an understanding of "church" can be valid as long as it is not the *only* way of belonging and of being church. The New Testament also speaks of a wider belonging, for example, to the church of a town or city which is characterized not by "likeness" but by "unlikeness" in terms of wealth or poverty, racial or religious background, etc. (1 Cor. 11:20-22; Gal. 2:11-16; James 2:1-7). The New Testament knows too of the church in a particular region, such as Judaea or Asia, presumably even more diverse than that of the city or town (Acts 9:31; 1 Pet. 1:1; Rev. 1:4; etc.). There is then the worldwide church of Ephesians and Colossians (Eph. 1:22; 3:10; Col. 1:18; etc.). Each such manifestation of the church, if it is faithful to the deposit of faith, partakes in that heavenly reality, the blessed company of all the faithful, Jerusalem our mother which is above (Gal. 4:26), to the extent that Christ is present in it.[11] Those then who would like to worship and have fellowship with others like them must also be committed to worship and have fellowship with those who are unlike them in ethnicity, caste, class, and even language. In Africa, for example, there is a tendency to have single-tribe dioceses. If a tribe is the only one in a specific area, there can, of course, be no objection to such an arrangement, but what if, as is often the case, there are others? Do they then ask for their own diocese or even province? A tribe should be able to express Christian faith and to worship in its own way and language but, at the same time, it must show itself as committed to the catholicity of the church by a wider belonging—for example, in a multi-tribe diocese—by accepting episcopal and local church leadership from others, and by regular worship and fellowship with Christians unlike themselves.

When to Say "Yes" and When to Say "No"

In the past, Christians have had to reject certain cultural practices in the name of the gospel. The practice of *Sati*—where usually higher caste Hindu widows threw themselves on the funeral pyres of their

---

[11]Nazir-Ali, *The Unique and Universal Christ*, 80.

husbands—was vigorously opposed by Christian missionaries, whose struggle also inspired Hindu reformers, and led the British to ban the practice in 1829.[12] Twin killing, similarly, in East Africa was opposed until quite recent times by missionaries, both African and others, as they sought to bring the gospel to those groups which practiced it. This was also the case with cattle stealing among the Masai on the grounds that all cattle belonged to them anyway and so to take other people's cattle was not stealing![13]

The question of polygamy has been much more controversial: Western missionaries in Africa, for instance, prohibited polygamous men from baptism unless they had put away all but one of their wives. This meant that those who were baptized had to send away their other wives, possibly into penury or even prostitution. Some who had considered the Christian faith found this demand impossible and either remained in their traditional religion or responded to Islamic *da'wa* and became Muslims!

David Gitari treats polygamy as a matter which the gospel can tolerate for the time being. Thus, in the Anglican Church in Kenya, polygamists can be baptized and confirmed, together with their wives and children. The expectation is that those already Christian will not take more than one wife. If they do, they will be disciplined, but pastoral care will still be available to them. Under Gitari's influence, although with opposition from some Anglican provinces in Africa, the 1988 Lambeth Conference passed a resolution which, more or less, reflected Gitari's position, while not endorsing his claim that the Bible does not clearly teach monogamy as God's purpose for men and women.[14]

In some cultures, even among Christians, arranged marriages are the norm. There is nothing wrong in the practice itself, and it has been shown to produce stable marriages, with a greater involvement of families than in marriages built on a chance meeting or on mere romantic feeling. There must, however, be the free consent which

---

[12]See further Kenneth Jones, *Socio-Religious Reform Movements in British India: The New Cambridge History of India* (Cambridge: Cambridge University Press, 1997), 30–1, 125–6.

[13]Gitari, "Evangelisation and Culture," 105.

[14]Gitari, "Evangelisation and Culture," 106–9, and Resolution 26 in *The Truth Shall Make You Free: Report of the Lambeth Conference 1988* (London: Anglican Communion Council, 1988), 220–1.

the church has always insisted on, and couples should not be pressured into marriage because of other agendas the families may have. In some of these situations, the family links are so strong that couples find it difficult to "leave and to cleave" and to become "one flesh" in the sacramental sense laid out in Paul's letter to the Ephesians (5:31-33) and ultimately based on the creation mandate itself (Gen. 2:24).

In the Western world today, it is most important to state and restate a properly biblical anthropology: God has made men and women together in his image. Together they have been given a common mission in the world, which divides into the mandate for procreation and family life and the wider mandate of stewardship in creation. Although they work in partnership and in mutual assistance, they each fulfil their role in distinctive ways which arise out of the way in which each is made. Their complementarity—biological, sexual, psychological, and social—is the basis of marriage and of wider relationships in church and society, where each functions in the integrity of his or her own being (Gen. 1:26-30; 2:18-24; Mark 10:6-9 and parallels; Eph. 5:21-33). This does not mean that roles are stereotyped, though that may happen in fallen cultures, but that each fulfils his or her tasks in ways that are distinctive and different.

The constructivism, so fashionable in the West, where people construct their own personal, gendered, sexual, and social worlds, regardless of the objectivity of their own beings and of the world, is decisively judged by such an anthropology, even if pastorally we may be called to exercise compassion for those confused about themselves or others by the culture around them that encourages people to relativize everything from sexual preference to the sanctity of the person at every stage of life.

We have seen, then, that inculturation or contextualization cannot be an unprincipled endorsement of every custom, value, or belief of a particular culture. It must proceed with certain criteria which spring from the gospel itself and it must work within certain limits which, again, have to do with the nature of the gospel, of the Christian community, and with the necessity of maintaining fellowship among the different communities set within very diverse cultures. From time to time, the evangelist and the pastor will, for the sake of the gospel, have to say no to aspects of cultures. This alerts us to the prophetic ministry of the church, both for Christians themselves and for wider society. Such a ministry should always be exercised in love, but it may need to critique the political and social life of a community in which the church finds itself, the institutional arrangements of the church itself, and even, from time to time, the values and lifestyles of Christians.

8

Prophetic Ministry, Social Responsibility, and Action

The church is a herald of the kingdom of God. It is not itself that kingdom in its fullness. Rather, it is part of the reign of God breaking into our world, and it shows forth the kingdom to those around it. As such, from time to time, it has to speak out and work for the kingdom and its values. Since the church must communicate divine truths to human communities, it looks supremely to the Bible and to the apostolic preaching for its understanding of human nature so as to convey its message effectively.

The Bible's anthropology is social from the beginning. Human beings are created male and female together. They are created in God's image for one another, and they are given two joint tasks, the procreation and nurture of children as well as the stewardship of creation, both to be undertaken together and yet each in his or her own way, according to the genius of each (Gen. 1:26-28; 2:23-25). In this sense, Christians can never be social contractarians. Their starting point cannot be individuals who, somehow, opt into social arrangements for mutual protection or prosperity. Even in a fallen world and among rebellious humanity, God has not withdrawn his providential grace and, to a greater or lesser extent, the essential structures of society—such as the family, arrangements for the defense and protection of citizens, provision for work, etc.—reveal something of a divine purpose in the ordering of society. While Christians witness to the kingdom of God, embodied in Jesus Christ and which is not of this world (John 18:36), they know also that the values of this kingdom have to be brought to bear on the kingdoms of this world so that they may approximate, more and more, to

God's will for them until they become the "kingdom of our Lord and of his Christ" (Rev. 11:15). Christian social witness and action is, therefore, rooted in a Christian vision of both the origin of society and of its goal.

Forthtelling and Foretelling

At first, Israel was under God's direct rule through the leaders he chose to raise up—that is, Moses, Joshua, and the Judges. Under Saul and permanently under David and his descendants, the original theocracy was replaced by a limited monarchy and by a separation of the spiritual from the temporal, of the priest and the temple from the palace and the king (Deut. 17:14-20; 18:1-8; 1 Sam. 10:25). The king and the court had specific responsibilities in governance, maintaining law and order, preserving peace on the borders, and waging war when that became necessary. The Levitical priesthood, on the other hand, was in charge of the sacrificial system, the thank offerings, and the maintenance of the priesthood itself. This separation of church from state is crucial for a biblical understanding of polity. It is true that in the course of history it was not always observed, with priestly families sometimes being de facto rulers of Jerusalem and beyond, as, in fact, they were in Jesus's day.[1] In the Bible, however, the distinction is maintained, even though church and state are closely related and are expected to work together for the common good (see, for example, the reforms under Josiah, 2 Kings 22–23, and also those of Ezra and Nehemiah; Jesus's cleansing of the temple may also, of course, be seen as a messianic and, therefore, royal act). This fundamental distinction between sacred and secular, and also their complementarity, is the background to Jesus's famous direction to render to Caesar what is (rightfully) Caesar's and to God what is (rightfully) God's (Matt. 22:15-22 and parallels). It is worth saying this because in many ancient religions, this distinction did not exist, as, indeed, it does not today in much Islamic polity.

---

[1] N. T. Wright, *Jesus and the Victory of God* (London: SPCK, 1996), 411, 541; Alan Runyan, "The Trial and Crucifixion of Jesus the Messiah" (unpublished, 2014), section 12.

The default position in the Bible and Christian tradition is respect for and obedience to our rulers. They are an important aspect of the providential ordering of society to reward what is good and to punish what is evil (Rom. 13:1-7; 1 Pet. 2:13-17). There are limits, however, to such obedience. There are times, as Niebuhr has pointed out, when Christians must say no to cultural, political, or economic demands made on them by the dominant culture, even when it is the governing authorities which have sought to enforce such compliance.[2] The early Christians who remained faithful often went to their deaths, or to torture and imprisonment, for refusing to sacrifice to the gods and the Roman emperor or, in some cases, simply for bearing the name "Christian." In the Persian Empire, similarly, the Greek historian Sozomen records the terrible persecution of the church under Shapur II, but many other instances could also be given. The reasons, usually, were a refusal to worship the *Shahinshah*, the Persian "King of Kings," and the Sun.[3] We must, therefore, say no to government when it coerces us to do something that God has forbidden or, conversely, when it forbids us to act in accordance with what God has revealed. This could be worship of the state's ideology, as in North Korea and even China; unjust discrimination against people of a particular race, as in apartheid South Africa; penal law arising from extremist interpretations of Shari'a; matters of life and death; the nature of our sexual being and its expression; and what we teach our children in many "permissive" societies. When and whether to say no is a matter for individual conscience but it can also be led by the position adopted by a community of faith or, indeed, by the wider community acting in consonance with God's providential purposes.[4] The courageous witness of the Confessing Church in Germany during the Nazi period is another example of a community of faith saying no to both the racist ideology and the absolute demands of the Nazi state.

---

[2]H. Richard Niebuhr, *Christ and Culture* (London: Faber & Faber, 1952), 45.

[3]Henry Bettenson, ed., *Documents of the Christian Church* (Oxford: Oxford University Press, 1974), 13–14; Charles Bigg, *The Epistles of St. Peter and St. Jude* (Edinburgh: T&T Clark, 1987), 29; and William G. Young, *Patriarch, Shah and Caliph* (Rawalpindi: Christian Study Centre, 1974), 21.

[4]Michael Nazir-Ali, *Faith, Freedom and the Future: Challenges for the Twenty-First Century* (London: Wilberforce Publications, 2016), 59.

The Barmen Declaration, which undergirded their communal life, and which was largely inspired by Karl Barth, rejected the idea of *Deutsche Christen* or "German Christians" as a racially defined group that owed ultimate allegiance to the German state. If the Confessing Church was the ecclesial expression of this resistance, surely the life, work, imprisonment, and manner of death of the great pastor and theologian Dietrich Bonhoeffer was the personal. Not only in his writings but in his suffering and eventual execution, he showed the cost of saying no to tyranny.[5]

Every Christian and the whole church have a responsibility to say yes or no to the demands of culture, polity, or even family, clan, and tribe. Those who are called to a ministry of teaching and leading, such as bishops and clergy, have, however, a special role in voicing the teaching of the Bible and of the church in particular circumstances. The biblical witness is that, in this context, God can call certain people to bear witness to his will. There is a continuity between both testaments in the bearing of prophetic witness and in the exercise of the prophetic office. In the Hebrew Bible, the prophet receives God's word through a vision, a dream, or the direct inspiration of the Spirit of God. This word is given so that it may be communicated to the people of God, those in authority, and even the nations roundabout. The word is a *forthtelling*, in speech or action, of God's will in a particular situation. This is not arbitrary or fickle but is always related to who God is, how he has made the world, and what are his expectations of humans in the choices facing them. The prophetical office is also about *foretelling*—that is, warning or promising what the future will look like depending on whether we choose to ignore or obey God's word to us. Once again, this is not magic or clairvoyance but insight about the future in the light of the word of God.

Old Testament prophecy continues in the New Testament in the person of John the Baptist or of Simeon or of Anna, but there is also the distinctive exercise of prophecy and the office of prophet in the new order (Acts 11:27-28; 13:1; 21:7-14; 1 Cor. 11:4-5; 12:10, 28; Eph. 2:20; 3:5; 4:11; etc.). There is no reason to believe that such a

---

[5]Eberhard Bethge, *Dietrich Bonhoeffer: A Biography* (Minneapolis, MN: Augsburg Fortress Press, 1999).

ministry is not needed any longer in the church. It is true that the closure of the biblical canon means that the teaching of the church and of its ministers must always be in agreement with it, but the very existence of a proclaiming and teaching ministry demands that the Scriptures and their teaching should be related to the varying circumstances and challenges of each age and culture.[6]

It would appear that the office of bishop developed not only from the need for the presbyters (or elders) of a local church to have a chairman but also from that of the apostolic delegates, Timothy and Titus, who had oversight of the churches of Ephesus and Crete respectively and responsibility for appointing presbyters, deacons, and others office holders (1 Tim. 3:1-13; Titus 1:5-9). Timothy is explicitly told to preach the word and to be urgent in season and out of season, fulfilling the work of an evangelist (2 Tim. 4:1-6). Clearly, there was fluidity in the early period of forms of ministry and the organization of local churches, but it was never just charismatic communities at first and then a gradual institutionalization. From the beginning, it seems, the apostles provided some kind of order for the churches founded as a result of their mission (Acts 6:1-6; 13:1-3; 14:23; 20:17-35; 1 Cor. 12:27-31; Eph. 4:11; 1 Pet. 5:1-4; etc.). Not only that, but the principle of *episcope*, or of oversight, however it is expressed, is embedded in the New Testament's ecclesiology.

Bishop Charles Gore, in his work *The Ministry of the Christian Church*, points out that in both the New Testament and the subapostolic literature, we find a ministry of "apostles and prophets" which is different from that of the presbyters/bishops (the terms "presbyter" and "bishop" are used interchangeably) and deacons, and supervisory of them. In the very early *Didache*, or *The Teaching of the Twelve Apostles*, the prophets, who are also called apostles, are allowed to say the Eucharistic prayer extempore and, if they settle down in a community, they are to be supported with the first fruits of the community for whom they are the "high priests." Such a localization of a hitherto itinerant ministry of encouragement and teaching, according to Gore, has also contributed to the emergence of the historic episcopate. Thus, the bishop is not just a fellow

---

[6]See further N. Hillyer, "Prophecy" and "Prophets," in *The Illustrated Dictionary of the Bible*, vol. 3, ed. J. D. Douglas (Leicester: IVP, 1980), 1276.

presbyter but is an apostolic delegate and has a prophetic mission and ministry.[7]

Presbyters share, of course, in the whole of the bishop's ministry, and that must include the prophetic and missionary aspects of it. In 1 Timothy 5:17, we are told that those stipendiary clergy who preach and teach are worthy of double reward. Such preaching and teaching would surely have included ministries both of foretelling and forthtelling. One of the Gospels set for the ordination of priests in the Ordinal attached to the *Book of Common Prayer* is from Matthew chapter 9, where Jesus asks the disciples to pray that God will provide laborers for the harvest that is ready. The ordaining bishop then tells those about to be ordained priests that they are to be "messengers," as well as stewards and watchmen. It is true that Anglican tradition has tended to emphasize the pastoral role of clergy, and this has been enormously beneficial for the congregations where they have worked, but newer ordinals are bringing back a sense of mission to the work of presbyters. The *Common Worship* ordinal of the Church of England tells us, for instance, that presbyters are to proclaim the gospel and "to resist evil, support the weak, defend the poor, and intercede for all in need." There is clearly a prophetic ministry here! In the Roman rite also the ordaining bishop prays that the newly ordained priest's ministry may be such that the words of the Gospel may reach the ends of the earth and transform the family of nations.

If Acts 6 is to be seen, as it is in both the Catholic and Anglican traditions, to be a prototype of the appointment of deacons, then it is clear that the meeting of material need was one of their prime responsibilities. As the case of the first martyr, Stephen, shows, this by no means excluded a vigorous defense of the gospel and a prophetic witness to the leaders of his own people (Acts 7). Nor did it exclude Philip, another of the seven, from exercising an evangelistic

---

[7]Charles Gore, *The Ministry of the Christian Church* (London: Rivington's, 1889), 276; Aaron Milavec, ed., *The Didache* (Collegeville, MN: Liturgical Press, 2003), 10:7; 11:3; 13:1. For a different view of the emergence of the episcopate from the presbyterate, see J. B. Lightfoot's famous appendix to his commentary on the letter to the Philippians: *St. Paul's Epistle to the Philippians* (London: Macmillan, 1903), 181. Richard Hooker appears to hold that bishops are fellow presbyters except in those things which pertain to their office: Hooker, *Laws of Ecclesiastical Polity*, ed. A. Pollard (Manchester: Fyfield, 1990), 185–6.

ministry on the very borders of the faith (Acts 8:5–40). The *Book of Common Prayer* Ordinal has the bishop telling the ordinand that among the tasks of a deacon is to "search for the sick, poor and impotent people of the parish" so that they are relieved of their needs. In *Common Worship*, this is strengthened to include not only the proclamation of the gospel in word and deed but to search out for the sick and lonely, the oppressed, and the powerless. The Roman rite also speaks of a concern for the sick and the poor and a zeal for the afflicted as aspects of diaconal service. Once again, there is clearly a ministry to the marginalized in mind here, and, from time to time, this must include ministries of encouragement and prophetic engagement.

Many church traditions have established, and are developing, bodies of social teaching which attempt to provide a common mind, or at least a common starting point, for thinking about the vital social, economic, and political issues of the day. The Roman Catholic Church's long tradition in this area—which stretches back to the debates about the fundamental rights of the indigenous people of the Americas held between the Dominicans and the so-called Humanists in the sixteenth century, and back to St. Thomas Aquinas himself—is well summed up in the Second Vatican Council's *Gaudium et Spes* ("Pastoral Constitution on the Church in the Modern World").[8]

Social Concern and Social Action

The Anglican tradition also has a long history of social concern. From the beginnings of Anglican reform, Poor Laws were framed on a national scale, with the parish as the focus and agent of delivery for poor relief. *Mutatis mutandis*,[9] these continued in place until the nineteenth century when they were replaced by the "workhouse"

---

[8]Austin Flannery OP, ed., *Vatican Council II: The Conciliar and Post Conciliar Documents* (Northport, NY: Costello, 1987), 903; and Roger Ruston, "Theologians, Humanists and Natural Rights," in *Religious Liberty and Human Rights*, ed. Mark Hill (Cardiff: University of Wales Press, 2002), 14–44.

[9]That is, "with the necessary adjustments to fit evolving circumstances having been made."

laws. In the 1547 Injunctions of the boy-king Edward VI (reigned 1547–1553), congregations were ordered to install what the *Book of Common Prayer* came to call "the poor men's box" near the high altar so that parishioners, in addition to their tithes, could now also give "to help the poor and needy, knowing that to relieve the poor is a true worshipping of God . . . and that also, whatsoever is given for their comfort, is given to Christ himself, and so is accepted of him."[10]

Two centuries later, the evangelical movement, similarly, had an outstanding commitment to social issues, working for the amelioration of the conditions in which the poor lived and worked, for the abolition of slavery and the evil trade which went with it, and for universal education. Such involvement went hand in hand with *postmillennial* views of Christ's return, holding that the proclamation of the gospel would usher in an age of prosperity and then Christ would return. It was incumbent upon believers, therefore, to work for such an age in preparation for his return. During the course of the nineteenth century, this belief was replaced by *premillennialism*, which declared that Christ would return first and then usher in his kingdom of love, justice, and peace. This, plus a rejection of liberal Protestantism's facile optimism regarding human progress, led to the evangelicals' withdrawal from the social and political scene. It was only at the Lausanne Congress of 1974 that evangelicals, once again, were able to affirm their commitment to sociopolitical involvement and responsibility, even if the extent and form of it was debatable and debated.[11] The report of a follow-up conference at Grand Rapids, Michigan, reaffirmed Lausanne in declaring that evangelism and social responsibility, while distinct, were integrally related in the proclamation of the whole gospel. Questions remained, however, as to whether this was just about social service or included action to challenge injustice, discrimination, and exploitation. There was disagreement also about the role of churches in anything that went

---

[10]For the Injunctions, see J. E. Cox, *The Miscellaneous Writings and Letters of Thomas Cranmer* (Cambridge: Parker Society, 1846), 503. For its role in Cranmer's *Book of Common Prayer*, see F. E. Brightman, *The English Rite* (London: Rivington's, 1915), vol. 1: lxix, cv; vol. 2: 662–3.

[11]David Bebbington, *Evangelicalism in Modern Britain: A History from the 1730s to the 1980s* (London: Unwin, 1989), 20; John Stott, *The Lausanne Covenant: An Exposition and Commentary* (Wheaton, IL: Lausanne Committee, 1975).

beyond service or whether that should be left to the well-formed consciences of individual believers.[12]

Since the beginning of the Lambeth Conferences in 1867, the Anglican Communion has also developed social teaching in a number of areas. The preparatory documents, reports, and resolutions of the conferences reveal a concern for a wide range of issues from discrimination and torture to disarmament and ecology. There has been teaching on the family, on contraception, and on human sexuality. Conferences have given attention to matters of human development and to economic systems, to drug and alcohol abuse, to gambling, and to trafficking.[13] An abiding problem has been that, because of notions of the radical autonomy of the Provinces, important aspects of such teaching have either not been received or have been openly flouted, leading to division, without any adequate way of resolving the problem and healing the division.

One feature of much church teaching in the area of social responsibility has been the use of the method of developing a common mind on the critical issues of the day and disseminating such a consensus among the members of the churches and sometimes beyond that. The methods developed in the early part of the last century by the emerging ecumenical movement among the churches, especially in the Life and Work Movement and Archbishop William Temple's Conference On Christian Politics, Economics and Citizenship in Birmingham in 1924, concentrated on building a common mind among people from diverse Christian traditions. Temple's way was to develop "Middle Axioms" which stood between fundamental theological convictions and action in Parliament, on the shop floor, or in the street. In the United Kingdom, this approach was hugely successful in the creation of a consensus which led to the creation and the sustaining of the welfare state (a phrase we may owe to Temple).

From the 1960s, however, many Christians in Africa, Asia, and Latin America began to criticize this approach as tilted toward those already with power, seeking to modify their thinking and

---

[12]See further Lausanne Committee for World Evangelisation and the World Evangelical Fellowship, *Evangelism and Social Responsibility: An Evangelical Commitment* (Exeter: Paternoster, 1982).

[13]For a convenient collection, see Roger Coleman, ed., *Resolutions of the Twelve Lambeth Conferences 1867–1988* (Toronto: Anglican Book Centre, 1992).

hoping thereby to ameliorate the lot of the poor and the powerless. They wanted to organize for "direct action" in changing the situation of the poor. The focus of much of this agitation was the continued survival of apartheid in South Africa, which legally and socially discriminated against the black and other non-white groups in the country, while privileging the whites in every area of life. Rampant inequality in South America, the paucity of clergy in the Roman Catholic Church there, along with a desire among lay people to be authentically "church" themselves, all led to the emergence of the basic communities. These Basic Church Communities (BCCs) organized for worship, supported their members in their needs, and prepared to be advocates for them in public life. In parts of Asia also, rapid urbanization had led to the emergence of an underclass whose cries of suffering were seldom heard by Christian leaders trying to interact with the wealthy and the powerful. Church organizations, like the World Council of Churches (WCC), began to make direct grants, for example, to liberation movements in Southern Africa. Liberation theology became the rage in both Western and non-Western theological circles. It is true that many of the liberation movements supported by the WCC—for example, in Southern Africa—have become the governments in the countries of the region. At the same time, some have, themselves, become corrupt and totalitarian—classic cases of the oppressed becoming the oppressors. David Martin, and others, have shown that, in Latin America at least, despite their emphasis on personal conversion and discipleship, Pentecostals and evangelicals are bringing about social change in ways that the BCCs have not been able to because the latter have not given enough attention to people's spiritual motivation.[14]

After Lausanne and its follow-up, a number of evangelical groups in different parts of the world have begun to take up the agenda of an integral proclamation of the gospel which included evangelism

---

[14]Michael Nazir-Ali, *The Unique and Universal Christ: Jesus in a Plural World* (Milton Keynes: Paternoster, 2008), 104; William Temple, *Christianity and Social Order* (London: Shepheard-Walwyn, 1976); David Martin, *Pentecostalism: The World Their Parish* (Oxford: Blackwell, 2002), 71; and "Justice," "Programme to Combat Racism," and "Just, Participatory and Sustainable Society," in the *Dictionary of the Ecumenical Movement*, ed. Nicolas Lossky (Geneva: World Council of Churches, 1991).

and church planting, social service, and, when necessary, challenging the powers that be on questions of fundamental freedoms, equal citizenship for all, democracy, and corruption. They have also rejected the Western bifurcation of evangelism and social concern and are building churches and institutions which embody such a holistic approach. This has given them credibility, beyond their numbers and resources, not only with local people but also with those involved in public life who cannot afford to ignore the significant change taking place on their doorsteps.[15]

In a world of growing hostility to the Christian faith—whether that arises from religious ideology, chauvinistic nationalism, or, as in the West, "liberal" intolerance—the prophetic witness of the church and of Christians will be more and more needed. It is part of the task of mission formation in our churches today to equip clergy and lay people not to shrink from such witness when it is required, even if the result is exclusion and persecution.

---

[15]Nazir-Ali, *The Unique and Universal Christ*, 112.

9

Why Evangelize and What Is Evangelism Anyway?

It used to be a standard dictum by the UK Home Office, in refusing overseas applications for asylum from members of the mainline churches, that such Christians cannot be persecuted because they don't evangelize! In such a view, it is only "evangelicals" who evangelize and can, therefore, be threatened by repressive states. Having seen, then, the different aspects of mission in presence and peregrination, identification and dialogue, prophecy and action, the question arises: Is there any need for intentional evangelism? By "intentional evangelism," we mean the sharing of the good news of salvation through word and act, through literature, drama, and film, with a view to bringing people to faith in what God has done through Jesus Christ in reconciling us to him when we were stuck fast in ignorance and rebellion (2 Cor. 5:19-21). Is this aspect of mission necessary with all the others? Indeed, is it the foundation of mission itself without which mission would be like a house built on sand, weak and incomplete?

What Is Evangelism?

One reason for rehearsing God's mighty works in history, especially in the person of Jesus Christ, is so that people may be reminded of who God intended them to be, so that his grace can draw them back to their true meaning and purpose through repentance. *Remembrance* is an especially important term in both testaments. Words derived from the root *zakar* provide different shades of meaning for remembrance. It can mean remembering God's mercies to his people. It can mean bringing the people to God's remembrance, and it can mean reminding God of what he has done and pleading that he might not forget his people now. *Anamnesis*, similarly, can mean both a remembering and a reminding, a recalling of a past event so that it may be made effective in the present.

For our purposes, evangelism is about reminding people of their dignity and worth as made in God's image but which is marred, obscured, and forgotten because of human waywardness, obstinacy, and rebellion. Kenneth Bailey, in his inimitable way, has pointed out how this emerges in the parable of the prodigal in Luke 15. Because of his adversity, the son "came to himself" (ESV) or "came to his senses" (v. 17 NIV). Bailey points out that the Syriac has "he came to his *nefesh*" (i.e., he came back to his own self). The old Arabic translations and commentaries agree. The son remembered what he had been and could see what he had become. This recognition of his fundamental estrangement from his true self can be seen as the beginning of repentance, but the climax is not reached, according to oriental commentators, until his experience of the father's unconditional love and his restoration to sonship. Having recognized the depth of his need, he discovered in his father's arms the love which alone had the power to make him whole. *Anamnesis* then leads to *metanoia*, to a complete turning around toward God, the very source of our being and our well-being. As with the prodigal, we are restored to our rightful place in the scheme of things and can begin anew to live as we were always intended to.[1]

Repentance, moreover, is not just about the initial repentance involved in coming to faith. As Christians, we continually need to repent when we have sinned and our relationship with God is damaged so that we may be restored to wholeness and fellowship with the one to whom we owe our very being and our salvation. That is why the opening sentences in the *Book of Common Prayer* Order for Morning and Evening Prayer include this quotation from 1 John 1:8-9: "If we say we have no sin, we deceive ourselves, and

---

[1]Kenneth Bailey, *Poet and Peasant and Through Peasant Eyes: A Literary-Cultural Approach to the Parables in Luke* (Grand Rapids, MI: Eerdmans, 1985), 173–4; Michael Nazir-Ali, *The Unique and Universal Christ: Jesus in a Plural World* (Milton Keynes: Paternoster, 2008), 117.

the truth is not in us, but if we confess our sins he is faithful and just
to forgive us our sins and to cleanse us from all unrighteousness."
The Confession and Absolution for Morning and Evening Prayer
and the Eucharist put this understanding of repentance at the very
heart of Anglican heritage spirituality. Repentance begins with daily
admitting to God the full range of our sinful choices: "We
acknowledge and bewail our manifold sins and wickedness, which
we from time to time most grievously have committed, by thought,
word and deed, against thy divine Majesty"; "we have erred and
strayed from thy ways, like lost sheep"; "we have followed too
much the devices and desires of our own hearts"; "we have offended
against thy holy laws"; "we left undone those things which we
ought to have done, and we have done those things which we ought
not to have done." We admit to God that we are estranged from
him, because our sins have "[provoked] most justly thy wrath and
indignation against us"; but we also have to face the harsh truth
that we are estranged from what God created us to be. In fact, we
are so far from our true selves that we have no power now in
ourselves to help ourselves be anything different. We can only cry
out to God that "there is no health in us." As the reality of our
situation sinks deep within us, "the remembrance of [our sins] is
grievous unto us, the burden of them is intolerable." We are indeed
"miserable offenders," people who have been made miserable by
our sins. "Penitent," we "earnestly repent"—that is, we are "heartily
sorry" for both where we are now and our choices which have
brought us to his point. Like the prodigal, our only hope is to return
to the unconditional love of our heavenly Father for us as shown in
Jesus Christ. Because of his love, not because of anything in us, we
turn to him, fully trusting him to both "pardon and deliver" us from
all our sins—that is, not only to forgive us of our sinful actions but
also to enable us to overcome the power of sin which still seeks to
be at work in us. That's why the priest or bishop asks that God give
us the gift of "true repentance and his Holy Spirit," in order to
"confirm and strengthen [us] in all goodness." For only by God's
renewing a right spirit in us through the gift of his Spirit at work in
us can we "live a godly, righteous, and sober life," where "those
things may please him which we do at this present, and that the rest
of our life hereafter may be pure and holy." In short, we ask God to
give us the gift of repentance that "we may ever hereafter serve and
please thee, in newness of life, to the honor and glory of thy name."

It is noteworthy that these texts have now been incorporated in the Catholic Ordinariate's *Book of Divine Worship*. The Catholic-Lutheran agreement on Justification also refers to 1 John 1:8-10 as a basis for the legitimate use of the term *simul justus et peccator* ("at the same time justified and yet sinful"), even if the two traditions approach the matter in different ways.[2]

Repentance and penitence get a bad press these days as somehow puritanical and life-denying, but in the Bible repentance is something positive, not only a turning away from what is harmful to us but a turning *toward* what is good, healthful, and life-giving. It is not about feeling worthless and seeking worth through someone's approval of us and our actions. It is rather precisely to know our essential worth before God and yet know also how far short we have fallen of God's purpose for us. It is to open ourselves again to God and seek his help to be what he wants us to be. It is the proclamation and the hearing of the gospel which makes repentance possible, and it is repentance which leads to "believing" the gospel as wholeness and fullness of life for us (Mark 1:15).

Humans are, by nature, spiritual beings who seek ultimate explanations for the existence of the universe and of themselves, and cannot forever be satisfied with mere description posing as explanation. Once they realize that the explanation lies outside of themselves and the immediately observable world, they are led to attitudes of wonder, reverence, and worship toward such a cause of theirs and everything else's being. However much material distractions, damaging relationships, and self-centeredness suppress this aspect of their nature, they are, in the end, *homo adorans*, made for worship either of the true and only God or of a substitute conjured up by human ingenuity or an aspect of creation worshiped in place of the Creator (Rom. 1:25).

In other words, human beings have spiritual aspirations which find expression not only in a religious tradition but also in music, poetry, literature, and history. To a greater or lesser extent, these aspirations are also affected by our fallen state and can be misstated or misdirected away from their true end. It is very difficult to

---

[2] *The First and Second Prayer Books of King Edward VI* (London: Everyman, 1968), 348–9; Ordinariates Established by *Anglicanorum Coetibus, Divine Worship* (London: CTS, 2021), 371–3; and the Roman Catholic Church and the Lutheran World Federation, *Joint Declaration on the Doctrine of Justification* (Grand Rapids, MI: Eerdmans, 2000), 43–4.

disentangle what is the authentic basis of such aspirations and what are false accretions. It is possible to say, however, that the coming of the gospel, in due course, reveals and judges whatever is false and idolatrous, but it also fulfills whatever drives people toward the truth of their Creator and a sense of their own destiny. As we have seen, Dan Strange, relying on Hendrik Kraemer, uses the term *"subversive fulfillment"* in terms of the Christian faith's relation to other religions: the genuine in place of the distorted, the real instead of the shadow, what is found rather than what is sought by human effort alone. What is said about religion, however, can also be said about other areas of human activity which seek to reach out to the transcendent who is also the ground of our being.[3]

It is undoubtedly the case that when people come to faith in Christ from a specific spiritual tradition, they see both that much has to be cast aside, if they are to follow Christ faithfully, but there is also that which is seen as leading them to Christ. This may be some element in their religious practice, or their previous scripture, or even their questioning of the tradition in which they stood. Subversive fulfillment seems an apt term to apply to both the positive and negative sides of their spiritual beliefs and aspirations before conversion. It is the sharing of the good news, however, and their acceptance of it which leads to their perception that all their authentic spiritual aspirations and hopes have been fulfilled in Christ. This is the personal dimension of the cosmic doctrine set out in Ephesians 1:10 that God is bringing to a head (*anakephalaiosis* or "recapitulation") in Christ everything that is in the heavens and on the earth. Thus, in Christ God fulfills his plan for the cosmos and brings it to its true destiny. It is well known that St. Irenaeus develops this Pauline teaching and, in addition to the fresh start to the cosmos in the incarnation, there is also the summing up and the renewing of humanity in Christ which is central to his teaching in this area.[4] If the gospel is not proclaimed, then, at the very least, we can say that the deepest longings of the human heart and mind remain unfulfilled.

---

[3]Dan Strange, *For Their Rock Is Not Like Our Rock: An Evangelical Theology of Religions* (Nottingham: Apollos, 2014), 266ff.
[4]St. Irenaeus, *Proof of the Apostolic Preaching*, trans. J. P. Smith (New York: Paulist Press, 1952), 30, 51, 67, and passim, Nazir-Ali, *The Unique and Universal Christ*, 119–20.

Assurance and Faith Working Out in Love

The sharing of the gospel does not lead only to our recognition of our true destiny and how far we have fallen short of it. It is not even just about our turning again from darkness to light, from self-loathing to a healing love. It does not only fulfill our deepest spiritual longings. It is about the *assurance* of our final safety in the hands of our Father, revealed to us in Jesus Christ. We need to know that in Christ the suffering of God has overcome our enmity with him, recreated a humanity in fellowship with him, thus dealing with the root of our and the world's suffering. He is faithful and calls us to faithfulness in obedience and trust (Rom. 8:18-39; Heb. 6:1-12). The Bible tells us that we have been saved (Eph. 2:5, 8-9) and are already seated with Christ Jesus in the heavenly places. Jesus, the Good Shepherd, assures us that he will not drive away anyone who comes to him, that he will never lose anyone in his care, and that he will raise them up at the last day (John 6:35-40; 10:4, 9, 14-16, 27-30). Those who put their trust in Jesus and in what he is and has done for them are already in a place of eternal safety. But this salvation also has to be worked out in our daily living, knowing how weak we are and continually invoking God's promise for ourselves and for those around us to change us from the inside out (Phil. 2:12-13). Finally, the salvation we know now in Christ is to be gloriously completed in the day of Christ's return. We hope but with certainty based on Jesus's own resurrection from the dead.

Such assurance does not stand alone, of course. In Reformed thinking, it must be accompanied by right belief, love of neighbor, and right conduct (e.g., as in 1 John). Pope Benedict XVI, in his lectures on Paul, tells us that Luther's teaching regarding justification by faith alone is true, if it is not opposed to faith working out in love (Gal. 5:6). According to him, faith is entrusting ourselves to Christ, resulting in being united with him and conformed to him who is himself love. In such fellowship with Christ, faith generates love toward God and our fellow human beings and thus brings about a fulfillment of the law.[5]

---

[5]Benedict XVI, *Paul of Tarsus* (London: CTS, 2009), 96ff.

This is the biblical faith which is our godly heritage. Ashley Null tells us, the English Reformers also believed that "to encounter unconditional divine love was to discover something deep within being touched—an unquenchable, often unexpected longing for a relationship with one's Maker being stirred up; a transforming grateful human love for God being gently drawn out; and a fervent drive to express this love in all outward actions rising up and directing the remainder of their lives."[6] They insisted on the Pauline doctrine of justification by faith, because only the assurance of divine love made known in free pardon through Jesus Christ had the power to produce such an inward, all-encompassing transformation in human hearts.

Occasions for Witness

For all of these reasons, evangelism is a necessary aspect of the church's mission. Indeed, we could say that presence, engagement, dialogue, social service, or action are not complete unless there is also an occasion for witness. This does not mean, and cannot mean, that people's access to what the church may have to offer in terms of education, material help, or advocacy is somehow conditional on hearing and accepting the gospel. Such conditionality would be proselytism and not authentic evangelism. It *does* mean that people should know why Christians and the church are involved in serving their fellows.

How, then, is such evangelism to be carried out by individuals, in homes, by agencies, and by the local church? There are numerous occasions in our working lives, during travel, or even at times of leisure, when something is said, a need is expressed, or a question is asked which can lead to witness about why we are working in a certain way, refusing a bribe, or not joining in the belittling of a colleague. I have often had to answer questions about why the church is involved in education or Christian agencies in medical

---

[6]Ashley Null, "*Sola Gratia,*" in *Reformation Anglicanism: A Vision for Today's Global Communion*, ed. Ashley Null and John W. Yates III (Wheaton, IL: Crossway, 2017), 110–11.

work. When people come to know about our faith, they may ask us to pray for them. If we pray in the name of Jesus for healing or for a good outcome of a difficult situation, this can lead us to asking them to put their trust in the God who loves us so much that he sent Jesus to heal us, feed us, and save us.

Christian homes are a key to hospitality. The opening of our homes to neighbors, friends, and colleagues, the use of a book, a film, or music which may result in discussion of creation, the uniqueness of the human person, or meaning and destiny can lead to sensitive but clear evangelism. The great days of the Christian calendar—Christmas and Easter, for example—can be used to draw others into our celebrations so that they can understand why we are celebrating and, if they wish, join in! Sometimes it is possible to comment even on the feasts of people of another faith. As Christians, we believe that God has a continuing and gracious purpose for the Jewish people which will reach its fulfillment in Christ (Rom. 9–11). There are several feasts and fasts of the Jews when Christians can explain, with sensitivity, what they mean to them. Thus, the relation between Passover and Easter can be discussed, or the relation between the Feast of Weeks and Pentecost, or the significance of the Day of Atonement (Yom Kippur). While the relation of the Jewish people to Christians is *sui generis* and cannot be replicated for another religious tradition, it is possible, in a more limited way, to do this, for instance, also with Islam. An example is the Feast of Eid al-Adha, which commemorates Abraham's (or Ibrahim's) preparedness to sacrifice his son in obedience to God. In the Qur'anic account in Surah 37:107, the boy is not named, and at the time of his deliverance, God ransoms (*fadinahu*) him with a "tremendous" sacrifice (*bdhabihin 'azimin*). There are at least two matters to note here: One is the notion of ransom through sacrifice, something missing from the rest of the Qur'an. The Qur'an denies that anyone can atone for the sins of another (6:164). Even the idea of one interceding for another is allowed only with reluctance (6:51, 70; 10:3; 19:87; 39:44, etc.). Yet here we have deliverance through ransom! Secondly, what is this "tremendous" or "great" sacrifice? It cannot be merely the ram caught in the bush by its horns of the biblical account (Gen. 22:13). Provided it is done with care and without triumphalism, such dialogue can be an important means of witness among our friends, neighbors, and colleagues.

The Congregation at the Center

While the witness of the individual Christian and of the household are very important for mission and evangelism, it would be the local congregation which should be at the center of this task. Bishop Lesslie Newbigin has written that the congregation is the only hermeneutic of the gospel.[7] The good news of the crucified and risen Messiah becomes believable in the world when a group of men, women, and children live it day by day in their life together. Even if we can argue that there are other effective interpreters of the gospel such as apologists, public intellectuals, and campaigners, we can agree with Newbigin that the congregation must be seen as being at the forefront of this task. So what should characterize a congregation that is seeking to be an effective interpreter of the gospel to the world around?

Newbigin begins with praise—that is, an acknowledgement of the goodness and beneficence of the one who is immeasurably greater than ourselves and who is continually at work bringing order out of chaos, beauty from ashes, redemption through suffering, and life from death. He is the origin of all those values about dignity, equality, and liberty to which the world pays lip service without acknowledging their source. As an Anglican bishop, Stephen Sykes, has said, it is those who praise God in the congregation who are most likely to praise him in the world.[8]

Newbigin turns next to thanksgiving as an aspect of the church's praise. As forgiven sinners who are constantly being renewed in our following of Christ and in receiving and using the gifts of the Spirit, we should be seen as a thankful people. The church's thanksgiving can take many forms, including giving for the mission of the church, to those in need, and as a vital aspect of prayer. From the time, however, that Jesus, before he suffered, took the bread and wine and gave thanks to God (*eucharisteo*), eucharist, or the giving of thanks, has come to be specially associated with the celebration of the Lord's Supper (Mark 14:22-24 and parallels; 1 Cor. 11:23-26). The early manual of Christian catechesis, worship,

---

[7] Lesslie Newbigin, *The Gospel in a Pluralist Society* (London: SPCK, 1989), 227.
[8] Stephen Sykes, "An Anglican Theology of Evangelism," *Theology* 762 (1991), 405–14.

and discipline—the *Didache*—uses this term both for the breaking of the bread and the thanksgiving following the receiving of the sacrament.[9] The Latin of the Thirty-Nine Articles also uses the term alongside the Lord's Supper (cf. the *Book of Common Prayer* term "Holy Communion," which has become the most commonly used term in the Anglican world). It is an appropriate word to use because as we remember and receive the benefits of Christ's sacrifice on the cross, we are moved to give thanks for all that God has done, but specially for what he has done in Christ. Here is the heart of the *Book of Common Prayer*'s theology as expressed in the liturgy— grace leads to gratitude. This giving of thanks, according to Paul, is also a proclamation (*katangello*) of the gospel (1 Cor. 11:26). It is not only an acknowledgment of God's graciousness to us but a means of witness to a watching world of what God has done for us and can do for them!

The congregation (and the wider church) is also a community of truth. It lives by, and assesses everything according to, the truth revealed by God to his people and definitively recorded in the Scriptures. It cannot, then, simply capitulate to the spirit of the age and its fashions but must maintain a critique of contemporary mores in the light of the gospel and its values. It is to be a community of love. Christians and the church cannot argue for a just and compassionate society if the church itself is not a fair and loving community. It must manifest at least a foretaste of the coming kingdom of God. Because it looks to the coming kingdom and the fulfillment of divine purpose, it stands over and against every denial of hope, and it rejects every worldview which sees the universe as meaningless and human life as futile.

Newbigin is alert to the need for the church to be prepared for such a mission of praise and thanksgiving, of truth and love, and of hope in human and cosmic destiny. Some years ago, I was asked by the General Synod of the Church of England to write a paper on the shapes of the church to come. In this paper, and the accompanying book, I set out ways in which the gifts given to each of the baptized need to be discerned and enabled. Those called to specific lay and ordained ministries also need adequate programs of formation for

---

[9]Aaron Milavec, ed., *The Didache* (Collegeville, MN: Liturgical Press, 2003), 9:1f, P23.

the ministry to which they have been called. Educators need to be educated and trainers trained! Only thus will the church be able to fulfill its missionary task.[10]

How, then, will such a church engage in its mission to those around it? Raymond Fung came from a background in Industrial Mission in Hong Kong. He was then the Evangelism Officer for the World Council of Churches until his return to Hong Kong. As a result of his experiences, Fung was much exercised by questions about what the wider community thought about Christians and the church. What were they about and was it at all relevant to them? As a result, he developed what came to be known as the Isaiah Vision. This was taken from Isaiah 65:20-23, which looks forward to a time when children do not die young. Older people live with dignity, as befits their age. Those who build houses are able to live in them, and workers benefit from the product of their work. For Fung, such a vision provides an agenda for the churches to invite others to join in working for the achievement of this vision. He claimed that others would find such an agenda attractive, and it would draw them into contact with a church. This could lead to witness as to why Christians have such an agenda and to celebrations, including worship, when landmarks are reached along the way. Such a process of working together, of witness, and of exposure to worship would be part of evangelization, leading people to faith and to discipleship.

I believe Fung is right about the attractiveness of such an agenda for many, but whether joining in a struggle for justice and for human welfare leads to faith and to discipleship is much more open to debate. As we saw during the Jubilee campaign at the turn of the new millennium, people were happy to join in a Christian and church-led campaign for the cancellation of the debt of poorer nations, but this did *not* lead them to becoming members of the church. Fung's agenda is attractive, nevertheless, and when Christians and others work together in these ways, who knows what God could do and what the result might be.[11]

---

[10]Michael Nazir-Ali, *Shapes of the Church to Come: Strategic Issues for the House of Bishops and the Archbishops' Council*, in the General Synod of the Church of England, Publication GS 1455; and Nazir-Ali, *Shapes of the Church to Come* (Eastbourne: Kingsway, 2001).

[11]Raymond Fung, *The Isaiah Vision: An Ecumenical Strategy for Congregational Evangelism* (Geneva: World Council of Churches, 1997).

Ann Morisy, a community theologian in London, in her book *Beyond the Good Samaritan*, has written that the church should not merely replicate what the social, medical, or educational services may be offering. There must be added spiritual value in witnessing to Christ, whether in the content of what is being delivered or in our attitude toward those needing or using the church's services or facilities.[12] So, a holiday club for children would certainly be educational and entertaining, but the material for stories, drama, or music may be drawn from the Bible or the heroic work of pioneers like William Wilberforce, Samuel Adjai Crowther, the Vietnamese martyrs, or the martyr-missionary Bernard Mizeki. Christian street theater, dance, and music have well-developed resources that can be accessed and used for work with people of all ages, as can films and books which pose important questions about life and death. An outing to the beach for older folk might end with a well-known hymn and a brief epilogue. Church halls, used by the wider community, will also have information to hand out about worship, study groups, and other church activity so a connection can be made, if people wish for such. A discreet and friendly presence of church members in and around the hall can also be helpful in giving advice, consoling the bereaved, or joining in a celebration. One way to engage the local community is to ask them what they expect the church to do for them. Experience shows that a variety of answers will be given. They may range from community use of the buildings for music or clubs of different kinds to a place for quiet reflection.

There may be a need for a place to meet to discuss matters of common concern, a center for advice, or a location for training programs in skills leading to employment. Any particular local church will not be able to meet every expectation and will have to prioritize what it can realistically deliver. Once again, the danger is of becoming simply a vehicle for social provision. If such an approach is to be taken, it must be with the full involvement of the congregation, with prayer and in partnership with Christian and secular agencies for the spiritual, social, and material resources which may be needed. Everything that is done should have a spiritual dimension to it.

---

[12]Ann Morisy, *Beyond the Good Samaritan: Community Ministry and Mission* (London, Mowbray, 1997).

Users of church facilities should be informed about the worship, fellowship, and discussion activities of the church and especially its work with children and young people. Wherever possible, there should be a Christian dimension to each activity, whether that is Christian music, traditional or contemporary, at a concert, starting and ending with prayer, an epilogue toward the end of an evening, grace before or after meals, an invitation to upcoming church events, or simply a visible presence to which people can respond, if they wish to do so.

Evangelism and Church Planting: Global and Local

At a global or national level, just adopting the secular world's agenda, even when it is desirable, as with the United Nations Millennium Development Goals, is not enough. As we have seen, true social and economic transformation comes about when people are challenged and changed from the inside. The growth of Pentecostalism in Latin America is bringing about social and economic change because people are living transformed lives. The East African Revival, similarly, has done more to change people's value system, leading to social and economic betterment, than any amount of top-down development plans. Even when cooperating with government and secular agencies in delivering relief, services, and projects, we need to seek to add gospel value to all we do. Our aim must be to address the whole person: spiritual, social, and physical.[13]

Sometimes, Christians and churches are shy of recognizing and meeting spiritual needs. The Anglican Church in Korea began some work with people who had moved into the cities for work and were living in large, unauthorized settlements. Because this is in relatively wealthy Korea, they cannot be called "slums," but they lack basic

---

[13]David Martin, *Pentecostalism: The World Their Parish* (Oxford, Blackwell, 2002), 83; Vinay Samuel and C. M. N. Sugden, eds, *Mission as Transformation: A Theology of the Whole Gospel* (Oxford, Regnum, 1999), 323; and Alison Barfoot of Uganda in personal correspondence with the author.

social services, educational facilities for children and young people, medical assistance, and even adequate sanitation. The Anglicans, along with other churches, began to offer employment advice, adult education, a place to meet, and nurseries for children, since both parents often have to work outside the home, etc. Gradually, the people began to ask, "Why are you doing all of these things for us?" When the answer was given, "Because we are Christians," they asked, "Why don't you worship with us then?" Thus, these "Houses of Hope," as they were called, also became "Houses of Worship"! The local residents began to take the lead in the services being offered and in the worship. As they came to lead, the agenda became more and more their own. They drew others into the worship and life of what was fast becoming a church, and so the house became a "House of Sharing," one of worship and of service.[14]

David Gitari and the Roman Catholic priest Vincent Donovan have drawn our attention to how both evangelism and church planting among the nomadic people of Kenya have to take account of their lifestyle, their daily routine, and their way of making corporate decisions.

Donovan, for example, visited the Masai communities early in the morning, before they went out to pasture their cattle, to tell them about Jesus. He then left them to think, *as communities*, about his invitation to become Christians. When he returned, most communities had decided to become Christians, but on the condition that *all of them* were to be baptized, not only those who had come to the early morning gatherings, on the grounds that those who had not attended were on community duties elsewhere and those attending had filled them in at the community's evening gatherings.

Gitari's strategy among the Gabbra is somewhat different: The evangelists, who are Gabbras themselves, are equipped with camels and goats. They join in with the people in searching for water and grazing areas. While traveling with them, they share the gospel with them. In the evenings, as the community gathers, the gospel is presented to the whole group, and there is vigorous dialogue between the evangelists and the gathered community. Gradually, this has led to the emergence of a church among the Gabbra and the

---

[14]Nazir-Ali, *Shapes of the Church to Come*, 103.

ordination of clergy from among them who continue to live in the Gabbra way and minister in culturally appropriate forms.[15]

The examples given above alert us to the need for culturally and contextually appropriate evangelism and church planting, whether it is among nomads in Africa or city-dwellers in Asia, wealthy suburbanites in the West or the marginalized anywhere in the world.

Church planting is often associated with primary evangelism and it can be so. There may also be other good reasons for it. For instance, a traditional congregation may want to start something for younger people away from traditional-looking buildings and trappings. A church in a commuter town has begun services in the afternoon for children who play sport on Sunday morning and for their parents and siblings. This takes place in a school hall, is quite short, and is followed by tea and cake! Many of these families are church families who are caught in a culture trap and are glad of being able to continue with some church connection, although new families can also be reached in this way. Sometimes, a church facility may be left unused in a particular area, and a nearby (or farther away) congregation may send in some volunteers to "kick-start" a congregation there, hopefully drawing in new people as well. These latter may be former church people who had fallen through the net somehow, or they may be new Christians who have been reached through Alpha, Christianity Explored, or Credo courses, or in some other way. In other situations, the denomination may wish to reach an unreached area and may be willing to put in human and material resources in terms of a ministry team, premises, and money.

From time to time, there may be theological reasons for planting. A group of Christians may feel that an area needs a church that expresses their style of worship or convictions, even if there are other churches in the area. In the Church of England, for example, an arrangement called a Bishop's Mission Order can now authorize church planting across parish boundaries where there is a distinct geographical area or a cultural group which the existing parish is unable or unwilling to

---

[15]Vincent J. Donovan, *Christianity Rediscovered: An Epistle from the Masai* (London: SCM Press, 1978); and David Gitari, "Evangelisation and Culture: Primary Evangelism in Northern Kenya," in *Proclaiming Christ in Christ's Way: Studies in Integral Evangelism*, ed. Vinay Samuel and Albrecht Hauser (Oxford, Regnum, 1989), 110–21. See also Gitari's autobiography, *Troubled but Not Destroyed* (McLean, VA: Isaac), 2014.

reach. Other denominations will have similar ways of accommodating innovative mission approaches. Internationally, as we have seen, the cell (rather than the home group) is structured to welcome new members, to evangelize, to disciple, and then to subdivide. This brings about rapid church growth, and some cells, or clusters of cells, can become the basis of a full-blown church plant.

Whatever model of church planting is used and whatever the need to which it is responding, it is important to count the cost at the beginning and throughout the process. Church planting is very much about carrying our cross in our following of Jesus, and so we should heed his warning about counting the cost of following him in this way. We should not be like the man who began to build a tower and could not complete it because he had not properly taken account of everything he would need to build it (Luke 14:27-30). Many church plants fail because there is not sufficient commitment among those who set out to plant: a few people in draughty premises, trying to improvise with the meager resources they may have for worship and fellowship, can soon start longing for the "fleshpots of Egypt" they have left behind, with rich liturgy, music, and like-minded friends! Many go back because they cannot cope with what they see as spiritual and social deprivation.

Whether it is a congregation or a denomination that is spearheading a plant, they must make sure that there are sufficient human and financial resources to carry it through. Misty-eyed romanticism about pioneering evangelism is not enough. Church plants also demand attention and time not only from those immediately at the coalface, but from leaders in the sending church or denomination. Given enough discernment of God's will, prayer, planning, and resources, however, there is no reason why a church plant should not succeed, but it does need much and enduring commitment.

Finally, it may be worth pointing out that while the term *evangelism* is understood to mean sharing the gospel with people in a way that brings them to commitment and the following of Jesus which that entails, *evangelization* is sometimes used to mean a continuing process of the gospel making us "gospel people." Christians and even church leaders, then, should be open to continuously being evangelized by the gospel in which they have put their trust (1 Cor. 9:16-27). Even as we evangelize, we are ourselves evangelized afresh by the gospel to which we bear witness (v. 23).

What Now Can We Do?

Looking again at the mission grid, we see that visible and credible presence is something to which churches and their leaders need to commit. Where there is a consecrated or dedicated building and its ancillaries, naturally, the question is how best they should be used and how they can signal an open and effective Christian presence. We have seen that while there can be hospitality for a range of social activities, we should aim to provide added value through Christians participating in them to the extent that they are able. Information about courses on Christian faith and life, worship, the Pastoral Offices, special events, and the church's involvement in local, national, and global issues can all be helpful in raising people's interest in Christian life and faith. In the organizing of services and other events, we should always have in mind how an "outsider" will view such events and whether the gospel will come through in a meaningful way for them.

In the dynamic ecclesiastical situation in which we find ourselves these days, however, there are many new churches and a number of older ones which have been deprived of their buildings by their parent denominations because of their faithfulness to the biblical and historic faith of the church. Such communities often find themselves using schools, clubs, and church buildings of other denominations. In such situations, it is vital that some sense of a continuing (that is, not merely episodic) presence is conveyed: for instance, by having a notice board outside which tells passers-by about the existence of the community and its programs of worship, welcome, and service. The use of social media can also be helpful in conveying such information.

Going out is as important as welcoming in, and churches of all kinds need strategies of visiting: whether that is existing church families or members, visiting homes of non-members in the neighborhood of the church to offer to pray with them, preparing people for baptism or marriage, or in the course of bereavement ministries. Processions on days like Palm Sunday or Good Friday, street theater, mystery plays or choreography, street book and music stalls, Christian "busking," etc. can all serve to keep the rumor of the gospel alive in the public spaces of our cities, towns, and villages.

We have seen already the importance of church planting in communities which are deprived of effective Christian witness. In some circumstances, intermediate steps may be necessary. These can take the form of opening a Christian home to hospitality-oriented courses like Alpha, RCIA, Christianity Explored, or Credo, which take place in the context of a meal. It can also mean offering help with schoolwork for children, providing advice on managing money, or organizing sports and youth clubs, where young people are offered friendship and skills which they desire, along with sensitive witness to the claims of the gospel.

Going out, of course, may mean going further than our street or town! It is important in our churches to discern how God is calling people and to what he is calling them. Some may be called to youth evangelism or to an itinerant sharing of the gospel cross-culturally. This may be to organizations like YWAM or Operation Mobilisation. Others may want to work with inner-city mission. In the UK, they may link up with an urban-based religious order, an agency like London City Mission or with SIM's cross-cultural initiative in Leeds. Those interested in parish-based missions could work with the Franciscans. Many mission agencies, orders, and coordinating bodies in the church encourage longer term commitment to mission service overseas, often in partnership with the local church but sometimes in pioneering situations. Sending agencies and churches now exist in many parts of the world, and the leaders of local churches should be aware of them so that those called to mission, in different ways, can be assisted by them.

As we have seen, embassy is a vital part of Christian mission, but so is hospitality, and the two need to be held in tension. One aspect of hospitality, which is coming strongly to the fore, is the need to welcome those from elsewhere who feel called to work on our patch, be it the parish, the diocese, or the national church. Such brothers and sisters may be called to work with a particular cultural group, their own or another one for whom they have a burden. *Partnership* between the local church and those who come is the key term, and it is good that mission and aid agencies, as well as bishops' conferences, have the expertise to make these links and to support the partnerships with training, counselling, and even finance.

However people are reached, it is important that they should not only be able to express their faith according to their own background and character but also be integrated into the life and worship of the local church. Integration does not, of course, mean assimilation. They should be encouraged to bring their riches to the local church, even as they receive from the local church all that it can give them. This will need much discussion, careful planning, and programming that is fair to all concerned.

Alertness to culture must be our watchword in our times! This has to do not only with exotic cultures we may find in our midst but with cultural change in the host culture as well. We need to be aware of how ideas about life, the universe, and our significance are changing. What is making people anxious? Who is lonely in the crowd? What are the patterns of addiction to dull the anxiety or the loneliness? What are the threats to healthy and life-giving relationships and what has the church to say about them? What is it that we can affirm in cultural change: concern for the rest of creation, a commitment to helping the poor, or being a voice for the voiceless, in our own community or beyond? What is it that we must resist and challenge: hedonism, consumerism, the deification of "nature," the fragmentation of the family, the lack of inter-generational communication, or reductionist attitudes toward the human person?[16]

What this critical engagement with culture brings us back to is the prophetical office of the church: in proclaiming the kingly reign of Christ and in setting forth his priestly work, the church will be called upon, from time to time, to speak out on issues that touch on God's providential care for human well-being and the common good (a ministry, if you like, of "forthtelling"). At other times, the church will need to point out the consequences of social, economic, and political decisions which may presently be obscured or neglected in society (the ministry of "foretelling"). This prophetic work of the church takes place at every level: global, national, and local. The local church and its pastors need to be aware of those developments in their communities, and even beyond them, which make for human flourishing and those which jeopardize it. They should be prepared to speak for the marginalized, the strangers, the allegedly unemployable, and the elderly, who cannot easily speak for themselves. They can also address global concerns of poverty, lack of religious freedom, the oppression of ethnic groups, the trafficking

---

[16]Michael Nazir-Ali, *Faith, Freedom and the Future: Challenges for the Twenty-First Century* (London: Wilberforce Publications, 2016), 37 and passim.

of women and children, and much else besides. We are fortunate that agencies like Tearfund, CAFOD, Aid to the Church in Need, Release International (Voice of the Martyrs), Open Doors, and many others can help us to do this.

The local church, then, as much as the national or the global, needs to be committed to the wholeness of mission. That is to say, the needs of the whole person—spiritual, mental, physical—must be recognized and addressed. Such a holistic approach is also necessary for communities in which a church finds itself. If there is a parish audit, for example, attempts should be made to at least name the felt needs of the community so the church can then prioritize, according to its resources, which it can begin to meet. This will certainly save it from the "navel-gazing" and inward-looking attitudes which can so often develop in congregations. The mission grid given in this book could also be useful for a local church to determine whether it is engaged in holistic mission and evangelism in its area and beyond. If it discovers that there are some areas missing or weaker than others, then there is opportunity to discover the resources and partnerships which might make them stronger or enable engagement in new ways of mission.

10

The Ordinariate

A Way to Unity?

How can *Ecclesia Anglicana*, as a whole, be renewed in such a way as to recover, once again, the mission of St. Augustine of Canterbury and his companions and that of the Northern Missionaries who also played a significant part in the evangelization of England? It is true, of course, that much depends on prayer for unity for the sake of witness to the world in tune with Jesus' own High Priestly Prayer as found in St. John's Gospel (17:20-23). With the help of the Holy Spirit, such a search must continue in patient dialogue between Christians of different traditions. Ecumenical dialogue assumes greater urgency, however, when it occurs between those Christians and ecclesial traditions which are of the same mind on crucial theological, moral, and ecclesiological questions facing the church today. In our context, this must be true of dialogue between the Catholic Church and those Anglicans who claim they believe nothing which the Fathers and the Councils did not believe or teach.

The emergence of the Ordinariates as a consequence of the Apostolic Constitution *Anglicanorum Coetibus* by Pope Benedict XVI is a most welcome development in that it allows those of Anglican heritage, who are seeking full communion with the See of Peter, to retain what is of value in their patrimony and, indeed, bring its riches to the wider Catholic Church. It is true that many Anglicans are seeking some kind of relationship with the Catholic Church because of a perceived lack of effective decision-making processes in the Anglican Communion, the absence, or near absence, of a commonly received body of teaching, and the need for an adequate teaching authority, which can, from time to time, declare the faith of the Church and how that relates to the day-to-day issues facing the faithful.

These are significant ecclesiological deficits but the Anglican tradition also has much of value in the beauty of its liturgical tradition, itself dependent on England's Catholic past and on the patristic church. Its valuing of the central role of the Holy Scriptures both in public worship and in personal and family devotion has led to an approach to the study of the Bible that is both scholarly and reverent. It is inductive, historical, literary, and canonical rather than deductive, speculative, and allegorical. It is committed to investigating what lies "behind the page" in terms of origin and intention but also to close attention to the text, as we have received it, and then relating it to the situation confronting the readers. The development of ministry in the Anglican context has led to an emphasis on a commitment to the wider community in which the church is set rather than just to the congregation. This has given the tradition some credibility in local communities and allowed it to develop its moral witness in a wider context. There is a whole corpus of theological, eccesiological, and historical work that is also of great value. There is much else to celebrate in music and hymnody, poetry and prose which have been given birth by this tradition.

The Apostolic Constitution recognizes these gifts and makes provision for their continuance and development in the Ordinariates. Development is, of course, a key term. A very good and worthwhile start has been made but the Ordinariates also need to develop in ways that are both distinctive and in harmony with the teaching and practice of the church down the ages and across the world. Particular attention needs to be given to the calling and formation of clergy so they are aware of Catholic teaching and their own patrimony. In practical terms, this means both studying with others training for the diaconate and priesthood and having their own adequate formation in the light of their heritage. It seems likely that clergy will continue to be received into the Ordinariates. How they are encouraged to *continue* in their ministry, in the light of Pope Paul VI's provision and permission in *Sacerdotalis Caelibatus* (42), will determine the future direction and development of the Ordinariates. How vocations are discerned and, as the Constitution and Complementary Norms affirm, men admitted to the diaconate and presbyterate, in consideration of Anglican ecclesial tradition and practice, will also affect the special character of the Ordinariates and influence its longer term future.

Again, in the light of Anglican practice, there is provision for consultation with clergy and lay people. This must develop, in full agreement with Catholic ecclesiology, so that every voice is heard but decisions are made, or advice given, according to the competencies of each segment of the Ordinariate, whether the Ordinary himself, the clergy, or the clergy and lay people together, without confusing their roles as has sometimes occurred in the Anglican Communion.

There is opportunity here to express a way of being Catholic which is in tune with the way in which the distinctive Anglican spiritual and intellectual heritage and discipline have developed and is yet in full accord with all the essentials of the Catholic faith.

In God's good providence, the Ordinariates can model a way in which different traditions may be "united but not absorbed," agreeing in all the essentials of the faith but also retaining all that is God given and valuable in their own history and heritage. It will be important, therefore, to include the Ordinariates in ecumenical discussion between the Catholic Church and other Christian communities, so that members of the Ordinariates can contribute from their own experience but also for them to learn from the opportunities and problems of ecumenical dialogue in our world today.

11

Summing It All Up

We have seen how the very origins of the *Ecclesia Anglicana* lie in mission and evangelism. Augustine's and his companions' mission from the south was complemented from the west and the north by Celtic missionaries evangelizing the north and even the Midlands of England. Anglo-Saxon missionaries, in turn, were central to the evangelization of Northern Europe. There were tensions certainly between the Celts and the Romans about church organization, the observance of festivals (especially Easter), ways of worship, etc. There were differences also between those who took a more positive view of culture and those who wished to destroy everything that smacked of superstition or idolatry. In spite of these differences, which today we would see as being about method and approach, the work of mission and evangelism continued because there was a common understanding of the meaning of the gospel and its implications for living the Christian life. These early missionaries and their converts also laid the foundations of Christian societies, which, whatever their faults, have given us our respect for the person, the institution of marriage and family, a common basis for law, government by consent, and much else.

We are indebted also to that great renewal and revitalizing of the church which took place, in different ways, during the sixteenth and seventeenth centuries. The Bible in the vernacular enabled people to sense God's judgment on human wrongdoing but also to know about the free gift of forgiveness and salvation through faith in the person and work of Jesus Christ. They understood how the law can show us where we have gone astray but cannot save us from the consequences of our lostness. When we are redeemed by Christ, however, we find that with the help of God's Holy Spirit we are enabled to see the law as a signpost for the ordering of our lives in Christ. A signpost we can follow with God's help.

Worship in the vernacular helped people not only to understand what was going on but to assent to it with their hearts and souls, as well as minds. There was a desire to engage all the senses of the worshipers—something we can do well to remember today as we seek to worship God with the whole of our beings. They sought also to disciple the whole nation into the way of Christ rather than to draw people into a narrow, sectarian understanding of the church. This approach has its dangers of accommodation to and compromise with culture, dangers we have seen dividing the churches in recent years. It is clear that the gospel must take precedence over inculturation. We cannot, however, deny the nobility of the ambition to reach whole nations. We have seen how the whole story of *Ecclesia Anglicana* provides a warrant for authentic inculturation.

The evangelical revival produced a great desire to evangelize people not only inside the church building but in the fields and streets and homes of a rapidly industrializing Britain. They were concerned not just with those of their own nation but with worldwide mission. They realized that the era of mission was not over and that God uses means (ourselves included) to reach others. The evangelical revival had enormous social consequences in England and its emerging empire: slavery was abolished; universal education—especially for girls—established; industrial legislation enacted to protect men, women, and children in the factories and mines of Great Britain; and a great deal besides. The Catholic movement produced a renewed sense of the spiritual identity of the church and of its calling to mission and the planting of churches in the neediest areas of Britain and, in due course, worldwide. Those in the movement were more alert to the dangers of compromise with culture and put the church's integrity above any dealings with the powers that be.

Today, the Christian faith is spreading quickly in East and West Africa, in South-East and East Asia, in parts of Latin America, and in the Pacific. In the Islamic world, Christians are witnessing bravely to their faith in often extremely difficult circumstances of restriction, discrimination, and persecution. In the West, wherever Christians have compromised with or capitulated to the spirit of the age, the churches are declining. However, those that have remained faithful to the Bible and the "Great Tradition" of Christian orthodoxy which the heirs of the Fathers and the Councils share are seeing their churches grow stronger in faith and discipleship, as well as in numbers.

As I have said in an earlier work, mission today is "from everywhere to everywhere." I praise God that this phrase has quickly become a catchword in mission-minded circles. We need the most suitable, the best equipped, and the most committed to carry out the tasks of witness, service, and evangelism in any given context, without regard to place of origin, color, or ethnicity. In many situations in the West, mission may be most effective if it is heard by the unreached in an *unfamiliar* voice which compels attention. We have seen how the Anglican Diocese of Singapore is noted for its outreach programs in neighboring countries for which it has some responsibility. Here missionaries from the diocese are working in countries with very different economic circumstances from their own, in the context of a major world religion, or where there is or has been a totalitarian ideology. Whatever our differences of churchmanship, we can surely admire and learn from the missionary fervor of these Christians. The diaspora of Asians, Africans, and Latin Americans in the West poses many challenges for the churches there, but it is also a means by which declining churches which have lost heart, and even the faith, can be strengthened and renewed for the task of mission. We need the testimony of costly witness, of expressing the faith in hostile contexts, of humble service, and of the voice of prophecy, if the West is to be evangelized and discipled. Pioneers from across the world are engaged on the frontiers of mission. They often find that those who come from other faith backgrounds or from sacramental cultures of reverence can be especially attracted to a liturgical tradition, with systematic Bible reading, with the observing of the Christian year and its feasts and fasts—provided these don't simply retain "a form of godliness," "denying the power thereof" (2 Tim. 3:5), but are means of grace in bringing people to Christ and nurturing them in their following of him.

We are truly learning to give as well as to receive in a worldwide fellowship where God has abundantly given his gifts to his servants for the building up of his church and for making known the good news where it is not known or understood as yet. There is a glorious history. Many difficulties and challenges lie ahead but, for those who remain faithful and willing, there remains the "hope of glory" that is Christ himself (Col. 1:27). In Christ and with Christ and through Christ, the future of mission and evangelism, we pray, will be as glorious as the past.

BIBLIOGRAPHY

Allen, Roland. *Missionary Methods: St Paul's or Ours? A Study of the Church in the Four Provinces*. Cambridge: Lutterworth, 2006.

Appasamy, A. J. *Sundar Singh: A Biography*. Madras: Christian Literature Society, 1976.

Assad, Maurice. "Mission in the Coptic Church: Perspective, Doctrine and Practice in Mission Studies." *Mission Studies* 4, no. 1 (1987): 21–34.

Bailey, Kenneth. *Poet and Peasant and Through Peasant Eyes: A Literary-Cultural Approach to the Parables in Luke*. Grand Rapids, MI: Eerdmans, 1985.

Barrett, D. B., G. Kurian, and T. M. Johnson, eds. *World Christian Encyclopedia*. New York: Oxford University Press, 2001.

Beaumont, Mark. *Christology in Dialogue with Muslims*. Oxford: Regnum, 2005.

Bebbington, David. *Evangelicalism in Modern Britain: A History from the 1730s to the 1980s*. London: Unwin, 1989.

Bede. *The Ecclesiastical History of the English People*. Oxford: Oxford University Press, 2008.

Bediako, Kwame. *Christianity in Africa: The Renewal of Non-Western Religion*. New York: Orbis, 1995.

Benedict XVI. *Paul of Tarsus*. London: CTS, 2009.

Bethge, Eberhard. *Dietrich Bonhoeffer: A Biography*. Minneapolis, MN: Augsburg Fortress Press, 1999.

Bettenson, Henry, ed. *Documents of the Christian Church*. Oxford: Oxford University Press, 1974.

Bigg, Charles. *The Epistles of St. Peter and St. Jude*. Edinburgh: T&T Clark, 1987.

Bock, Kim, ed. *Minjung Theology: People as the Subjects of History*. Singapore: Christian Conference of Asia, 1981.

Boff, Leonardo. *Church: Charism and Power*. London: SCM, 1985.

Brightman, F. E. *The English Rite*, 2 vols. London: Rivington's, 1915.

Buchanan, Colin, ed. *Modern Anglican Liturgies 1958–1968*. Oxford: Oxford University Press, 1968.

Buchanan, Colin, ed. *Further Anglican Liturgies 1968–1975*. Nottingham: Grove Books, 1975.

Budge, E. A. Wallis. *The Monks of Kublai Khan*. London: Religious Tract Society, 1928.

Busby, Russ. *Billy Graham: God's Ambassador*. San Diego, CA: Tehabi, 1999.

Cardinal Ratzinger. "Christ, Faith and the Challenge of Cultures," *Origins: CNS Documentary Service* 24, no. 41 (1995): 679–86.

Cassidy, Michael. *The Passing Summer*. London: Hodder, 1989.

Cassidy, Michael. *Footprints in the African Sand*. London: SPCK, 2019.

Chadwick, Henry. *The Early Church*, revised edition. Harmondsworth: Penguin, 1993.

Chadwick, Owen. *The Reformation*. London: Penguin, 1990.

Chapman, Colin. *Islam and the West: Conflict, Coexistence or Conversion?* Carlisle: Paternoster, 1998.

Coleman, Roger, ed. *Resolutions of the Twelve Lambeth Conferences 1867–1988*. Toronto: Anglican Book Centre, 1992.

Cox, J. E. *Writings and Disputations of Thomas Cranmer . . . Relative to the Sacrament of the Lord's Supper*. Cambridge: Parker Society, 1844.

Cox, J. E. *The Miscellaneous Writings and Letters of Thomas Cranmer*. Cambridge: Parker Society, 1846.

Cracknell, Kenneth. *Towards a New Relationship: Christians and People of Other Faith*. London: Epworth, 1986.

Cragg, Kenneth. "Islamic Theology: Limits and Bridges." In *The Gospel and Islam*. Edited by D. M. McCurry, 196–206. Monrovia, CA: Missions Advanced Research and Communication Center, 1979.

Daniell, David. *The Obedience of a Christian Man*. London: Penguin, 2000.

Davies, John D. *The Faith Abroad*. Oxford: Blackwell, 1983.

Dehqani-Tafti, H. B. *Design of My World*. London: Lutterworth, 1959.

Donovan, Vincent J. *Christianity Rediscovered: An Epistle from the Masai*. London: SCM Press, 1978.

Duraisingh, Christopher, ed. *Called to One Hope: The Gospel in Diverse Cultures*. Geneva: World Council of Churches, 1998.

Eliot, T. S. *Four Quartets*. New York: Harcourt, 1943.

Evans, G. R., and J. R. Wright, eds. *The Anglican Tradition: A Handbook of Sources*. London: SPCK, 1991.

Farquhar, J. N. *The Crown of Hinduism*. Oxford: Oxford University Press, 1913.

Flannery, Austin, OP, ed. *Vatican Council II: The Conciliar and Post Conciliar Documents*. Northport, NY: Costello, 1987.

Fung, Raymond. *The Isaiah Vision: An Ecumenical Strategy for Congregational Evangelism*. Geneva: World Council of Churches, 1997.

Gaudeul, Jean-Marie. *Encounters and Clashes: Islam and Christianity in History*, vol. 1. Rome: Pontifical Institute for the Study of Arabic and Islamic Studies, 1984.

Ghazzali, Al. *Mishkat Al Anwar* as the *Niche for Light*. Translated by W. H. T. Gairdner. London: Royal Asiatic Society, 1924.

Gitari, David. "Evangelisation and Culture: Primary Evangelism in Northern Kenya." In *Proclaiming Christ in Christ's Way: Studies in Integral Evangelism*. Edited by Vinay Samuel and Albrecht Hauser, 101–21. Oxford: Regnum, 1989.

Gitari, David. *Troubled but Not Destroyed*. McLean, VA: Isaac, 2014.

Gore, Charles, ed. *Lux Mundi: A Series of Studies in the Religion of the Incarnation*. London: John Murray, 1889.

Gore, Charles. *The Ministry of the Christian Church*. London: Rivington's, 1889.

Graham, Franklin. *Through My Father's Eyes*. Nashville, TN: Thomas Nelson, 2018.

Green, Michael. *Asian Tigers for Christ: The Dynamic Growth of the Church in South East Asia*. London: SPCK, 2001.

Griffith, Sidney H. *The Church in the Shadow of the Mosque*. Princeton, NJ: Princeton University Press, 2008.

Griffith, Sidney H. *The Bible in Arabic*. Princeton, NJ: Princeton University Press, 2013.

Hardwick, Charles. *A History of the Articles of Religion*. Cambridge: Deighton Bell, 1859.

Harris, Elizabeth. *What Buddhists Believe*. Oxford: One World, 1998.

Hefley, James, and Marti Hefley. *The Liberated Palestinian*. Wheaton, IL: Victor Books, 1980.

Hewitt, Gordon. *The Problems of Success: A History of the Church Missionary Society 1910–1942, vol. 1: In Tropical Africa, The Middle East, At Home*. London: SCM Press, 1971.

Hillyer, N. "Prophecy" and "Prophets." In *The Illustrated Dictionary of the Bible*, vol. 3. Edited by J. D. Douglas, 1276. Leicester: IVP, 1980.

Hooker, Richard. *Laws of Ecclesiastical Polity*. Edited by A. Pollard. Manchester: Fyfield, 1990.

Interfaith Consultative Group. *Communities and Buildings: Church of England Premises and Other Faiths*. London: Church House Publishing, 1996.

Ipgrave, Michael. *The Road Ahead: A Christian–Muslim Dialogue*. London: Church House Publishing, 2002.

Iqbal, Muhammad. *The Development of Metaphysics in Persia*. Lahore: Bazm-i-Iqbal, 1964.

Irenaeus. *The Proof of the Apostolic Teaching*. Translated by J. P. Smith. New York: Paulist Press, 1952.

John Paul II. *Slavorum Apostoli*, June 2, 1985, par. 21, *Acta Apostolicae Sedis* 77 (1985): 802–3.

John Paul II. "*Redemptoris Missio*: Encyclical Letter on the Permanent Validity of the Church's Missionary Mandate." *The Holy See*, December 7, 1990. *Catholic International* 2, no. 6 (1991): 275–7.

Jones, Kenneth. *Socio-Religious Reform Movements in British India: The New Cambridge History of India*. Cambridge: Cambridge University Press, 1997.

Ketley, Joseph. *The Two Liturgies . . . of King Edward VI*. Cambridge: Parker Society, 1844.

Kim Seng, Kuan. "Southeast Asia and Frontier Missions." In *Shadows from Light Unapproachable: Anglican Frontier Missions (1993–2018)*. Edited by Tad Bordenave, 131. Heathsville, VA: Northumberland Historical Press, 2018.

Kings, Graham. *Christianity Connected: Hindus, Muslims and the World in the Letters of Max Warren and Roger Hooker*. Zoetermeer: Boekcentrum, 2002.

Kinsella, W. P. *Shoeless Joe*. Boston, MA: Mariner Books, 1982.

Kraft, Charles. *Christianity and Culture: A Study in Biblical Theologizing in Cross-Cultural Perspective*. New York: Orbis, 1997.

Küster, Volker. "Visual Arts in World Christianity." In *The Wiley Blackwell Companion to World Christianity*. Edited by L. Sanneh and M. McClymond, 368–85. Oxford: Wiley, 2016.

Lausanne Committee for World Evangelisation and the World Evangelical Fellowship. *Evangelism and Social Responsibility: An Evangelical Commitment*. Exeter: Paternoster, 1982.

LeMarquand, Grant. "Bishop Grant & Doctor Wendy," http://www. grantandwendy.com/.

Lemon, Rebecca, Emma Mason, Jonathan Roberts, and Christopher Rowland, eds. *The Blackwell Companion to The Bible in English Literature*. Oxford: Wiley-Blackwell, 2012.

Lightfoot, J. B. *St. Paul's Epistle to the Philippians*. London: Macmillan, 1903.

Lossky, Nicolas, ed. *Dictionary of the Ecumenical Movement*. Geneva: World Council of Churches, 1991.

Lutheran World Federation and the Roman Catholic Church, *Joint Declaration on the Doctrine of Justification*. Grand Rapids, MI: Eerdmans, 2000.

MacIntyre, Alasdair. *After Virtue: A Study in Moral Theory*. London: Duckworth, 2000.

Massey, James. "Ingredients for a Dalit Theology." In *Readings in Indian Christian Theology*. Edited by R. S. Sugirtharajah and Cecil Hargreaves, 152–7. London: SPCK, 1993.

Marshall, I. Howard. *The Acts of the Apostles*. Grand Rapids, MI: Eerdmans and Leicester, IVP 1984.

Martin, David. *Pentecostalism: The World Their Parish*. Oxford: Blackwell, 2002.

Masry, Iris. *Introduction to the Coptic Church*. Cairo: Dar El Alam, 1977.

Mayhew, Peter. *All Saints: Birth and Growth of a Community*. Oxford: All Saints, 1987.

Mbiti, J. S. *African Religions and Philosophy*. London: Heinemann, 1969.

Mbiti, J. S. *Introduction to African Religion*. Nairobi: Heinemann, 1991.

Milavec, Aaron, ed. *The Didache*. Collegeville, MN: Liturgical Press, 2003.

Moorman, J. R. H. *A History of the Church in England*, 3rd edition. London: A&C Black, 1976.

Morgan, Robert, ed. *The Religion of the Incarnation: Essays in Commemoration of Lux Mundi*. Bristol: Bristol Classical Press, 1989.

Morisy, Ann. *Beyond the Good Samaritan: Community Ministry and Mission*. London: Mowbray, 1997.

Moule, C. F. D. *The Origin of Christology*. Cambridge: Cambridge University Press, 1990.

Moynihan, Brian. *William Tyndale: If God Spare My Life*. London: Abacus, 2003.

Murray, Jocelyn. *Proclaim the Good News: A Short History of the Church Missionary Society*. London: Hodder, 1985.

Nazir-Ali, Michael. *Islam: A Christian Perspective*. Exeter: Paternoster, 1983.

Nazir-Ali, Michael. *Frontiers in Muslim–Christian Encounter*. Oxford: Regnum, 1987.

Nazir-Ali, Michael. *From Everywhere to Everywhere: A World View of Christian Mission*. London: Collins, 1991.

Nazir-Ali, Michael. *Mission and Dialogue: Proclaiming the Gospel Afresh in Every Age*. London: SPCK, 1995.

Nazir-Ali, Michael. *Citizens and Exiles: Christian Faith in a Plural World*. London, SPCK, 1998.

Nazir-Ali, Michael. *Shapes of the Church to Come*. Eastbourne: Kingsway, 2001.

Nazir-Ali, Michael. *The Unique and Universal Christ: Jesus in a Plural World*. Milton Keynes: Paternoster, 2008.

Nazir-Ali, Michael. *Triple Jeopardy for the West: Aggressive Secularism, Radical Islamism and Multiculturalism*. London: Bloomsbury, 2012.

Nazir-Ali, Michael. *How the Anglican Communion Came To Be and Where It Is Going*. London: Latimer Trust, 2013.

Nazir-Ali, Michael. *Faith, Freedom and the Future: Challenges for the Twenty-First Century*. London: Wilberforce Publications, 2016.

Nazir-Ali, Michael. "How the Anglican Communion Began and Where It Is Going." In *Reformation Anglicanism: A Vision for Today's Global Communion.* Edited by Ashley Null and John W. Yates III, 15–44. Wheaton, IL: Crossway, 2017.

Nazir-Ali, Michael. *Shapes of the Church to Come: Strategic Issues for the House of Bishops and the Archbishops' Council.* In the General Synod of the Church of England. Publication GS 1455.

Neill, Stephen. *Anglicanism.* Harmondsworth: Penguin, 1960.

Neill, Stephen. *A History of Christian Missions.* Harmondsworth: Penguin, 1986.

Newbigin, Lesslie. *The Gospel in a Pluralist Society.* London: SPCK, 1989.

A New Zealand Prayer Book. Auckland: Collins, 1989.

Niebuhr, H. Richard. *Christ and Culture.* London: Faber & Faber, 1952.

Null, Ashley. "Divine Allurement: Thomas Cranmer and Tudor Church Growth." In *Towards a Theology of Church Growth.* Edited by David Goodhew, 197–216. Farnham: Ashgate, 2015.

Null, Ashley. "*Sola Gratia.*" In *Reformation Anglicanism: A Vision for Today's Global Communion.* Edited by Ashley Null and John W. Yates III, 110–11. Wheaton, IL: Crossway, 2017.

Ordinariates Established by Anglicanorum Coetibus. *Divine Worship— The Ordinariate Missal.* London: CTS, 2015, 2021.

Padwick, Constance. *Muslim Devotions: A Study of Prayer-Manuals in Common Use.* London: SPCK, 1961.

Palmer, Martin. *The Jesus Sutras: Rediscovering the Lost Scrolls of Taoist Christianity.* New York: Ballantine, 2001.

Pannikar, Raimundo. *The Unknown Christ of Hinduism.* London: Darton Longman & Todd, 1964.

Paul VI. *Evangelii Nuntiandi*, December 8, 1975, par. 53, *Acta Apostolicae Sedis* 68 (1976): 42.

Radner, Ephraim, and Philip Turner. *The Fate of Communion.* Grand Rapids, MI: Eerdmans, 2006.

Richardson, Don. *Peace Child.* Ada, MI: Bethany House, 2005.

Robins, Wendy, ed. *Let All the World: Liturgies, Litanies and Prayers from Around the World.* London: USPG, 1990.

Robinson, John A. T. *The Body: A Study in Pauline Theology.* London: SCM, 1952.

Rooney, John. *The Hesitant Dawn.* Rawalpindi: Christian Study Centre, 1984.

Rudvin, Arne. "The Gospel and Islam: What Sort of Dialogue is Possible?" *Al-Mushir: Theological Journal of the Christian Study Centre, Rawalpindi, Pakistan* 21, nos. 3–4 (Autumn 1979): 82–123.

Runyan, Alan. "The Trial and Crucifixion of Jesus the Messiah." Unpublished, 2014.

Ruston, Roger. "Theologians, Humanists and Natural Rights." In *Religious Liberty and Human Rights*. Edited by Mark Hill, 14–44. Cardiff: University of Wales Press, 2002.

Saeki, Peter. *Nestorian Documents and Relics in China*. Tokyo: Academy of Oriental Culture, 1937.

Saeki, Peter. *The Nestorian Monument in China*. London: SPCK, 1928.

Samuel, Vinay, and C. M. N. Sugden, eds. *Mission as Transformation: A Theology of the Whole Gospel*. Oxford: Regnum, 1999.

Sanneh, Lamin. *Whose Religion Is Christianity?* Grand Rapids, MI: Eerdmans, 2003.

Sanneh, Lamin. *Translating the Message: The Missionary Impact on Culture,* revised edition. Maryknoll, NY: Orbis, 2009.

Sharpe, Eric. *Not to Destroy but to Fulfil*. Uppsala: Gleerup, 1965.

Shenk, David, and Badru Kateregga. *Islam and Christianity: A Muslim and a Christian in Dialogue*. Grand Rapids, MI: Eerdmans, 1981.

Sider, Robert. *The Gospel and Its Proclamation: Message of the Fathers of the Church*. Wilmington, DE: Michael Glazier, 1983.

Siedentop, Larry. *Inventing the Individual: The Origins of Western Liberalism*. Harmondsworth: Penguin, 2015.

Snell, Margaret. *Bernard Mizeki of Zimbabwe*. Harare: Mambo Press, 1986.

Solomon, Sam. *Not the Same God: Is the Qur'anic Allah the Lord God of the Bible?* London: Wilberforce Publications, 2016.

Sparks, Adam. *One of a Kind: The Relationship between Old and New Covenants*. Eugene, OR: Pickwick, 2010.

Stacey, Vivienne. *Thomas Valpy French, First Bishop of Lahore*. Lahore: Masihi Isha'at Khana, 1979.

Stott, John. *The Lausanne Covenant: An Exposition and Commentary*. Wheaton, IL: Lausanne Committee, 1975.

Strange, Daniel. *For Their Rock Is Not Like Our Rock: An Evangelical Theology of Religions*. Nottingham: Apollos, 2014.

Sykes, Stephen. "An Anglican Theology of Evangelism." *Theology* 762 (1991): 405–14.

Taylor, John V. *The Go-Between God*. London: Student Christian Movement, 1995.

Taylor, John V. *The Christlike God*. London: Student Christian Movement, 2004.

Taylor, John V. *The Primal Vision*. London: Student Christian Movement, 2004.

Temple, William. *Christianity and Social Order*. London: Shepheard-Walwyn, 1976.

The First and Second Prayer Books of King Edward VI (London: Everyman, 1968).

The Truth Shall Make You Free: *Report of the Lambeth Conference 1988*. London: Anglican Communion Council, 1988.

United Nations General Assembly. *Universal Declaration of Human Rights*. New York: UN Office of Public Information, 1973.

Warneck, G. *Outline of a History of Protestant Missions from the Reformation to the Present Time: A Contribution to Modern Church History*. New York: Fleming H. Revell, 1901.

Wessels, Anton. *Europe: Was it Ever Really Christian?* London: Student Christian Ministry, 1994.

White, Andrew. *The Vicar of Baghdad*. Oxford: Monarch, 2009.

White, Andrew. *My Journey So Far*. Oxford: Lion, 2015.

Willett, Frank. *African Art*. London: Thames & Hudson, 1971.

Williams, Peter. *The Ideal of the Self-Governing Church: A Study in Victorian Missionary Strategy*. Leiden: Brill, 1990.

Worth, Jennifer. *Call the Midwife*. London: Orion, 2002.

Worth, Jennifer. *Shadows of the Workhouse*. London: Weidenfeld & Nicolson, 2005.

Worth, Jennifer. *Farewell to the East End*. London: Weidenfeld & Nicolson, 2009.

Wright, N. T. *Jesus and the Victory of God*. London: SPCK, 1996.

Young, William G. *Patriarch, Shah and Caliph*. Rawalpindi: Christian Study Centre, 1974.

GENERAL INDEX

SCRIPTURE INDEX

Qur'anic References